THE
SURREY
COOK BOOK

A CELEBRATION OF THE AMAZING FOOD & DRINK ON OUR DOORSTEP

The Surrey Cook Book

First edition printed in 2020 in the UK.

ISBN: 978-1-910863-50-3

Compiled by: Kathryn Dockerty, Jo Mallinder, Emma Toogood

Written by: Katie Fisher and Kate Reeves-Brown

Photography by:
Paul Gregory (paulgregoryphotography.co.uk)
Simon Weller (simonweller.com)
Matt Crowder (mattcrowder.co.uk)

Edited by: Phil Turner

Designed by: Paul Cocker, Matt Crowder

Contributors: Rupinder Casimir, Michael Johnson, Aimee Kirkup, Sarah Koriba, Paul Stimpson

Cover art: Luke Prest (lukeprest.com)

Printed by: Bell and Bain Ltd, Glasgow

Published by Meze Publishing Limited
Unit 1b, 2 Kelham Square
Kelham Riverside
Sheffield S3 8SD
Web: www.mezepublishing.co.uk
Telephone: 0114 275 7709
Email: info@mezepublishing.co.uk

CONTENTS

WELCOME TO SURREY

THE BEAUTIFUL COUNTY OF SURREY HAS SO MUCH TO OFFER, AND THE BRILLIANT BUSINESSES FEATURED IN THIS BOOK ARE JUST THE TIP OF THE ICEBERG...

Surrey is known for attractions such as the Area of Outstanding Natural Beauty in the Surrey Hills as well as nationally renowned landmarks like Hampton Court Palace and Richmond Park, but there's more to Surrey than first meets the eye. As one of London's neighbouring counties, Surrey shares much of the capital city's diversity and eclectic culture when it comes to food and drink, but also has its own unique characteristics that stand apart. For example, Surrey is England's most wooded county, making it the perfect setting for foraging and game hunting.

It has everything from cosy country pubs, exceptional afternoon teas, farm to fork dining experiences and next level street food. These are made possible by a host of amazing producers; the county is particularly renowned for farming fresh trout, watercress, game and livestock. And as of 2020 Surrey can boast four Michelin-starred restaurants, putting it firmly on the map for fine dining.

If your perfect meal out is a more relaxed affair, there's no shortage of food and drink-focused events throughout the year: the eponymous food festival held in Richmond, Guildford Cheese and Chilli Festival, BBC Good Food Festival and Woking Beer Festival all happen here. It also has an annual awards ceremony run by Surrey Life Magazine, whose previous winners include some of the fantastic businesses that you can find within this book: Dorking Butchers, Salt Box, Albury Vineyard and Secretts of Milford are all part of that culinary hall of fame.

To wash it all down, there are plenty of places to quaff quality drinks across the county including many of England's best vineyards. The recent rise in English wine has been spearheaded by Surrey, which produces sparkling wine to rival champagne right at its heart. The area also has its fair share of national award-winning gins - Silent Pool and Elstead distilleries fly the flag in this book - and the North Downs Way Ale Trail passes through a number of Surrey's finest breweries.

So what's in store for the future of this exciting county? Surrey's food scene and cultural landscape is set to continue growing, given a boost in 2019 by the first ever Surrey Day. This landmark event showcased the brilliant businesses, must-see destinations and special places to live and visit in and around the county. It offered people a great insight into the unique aspects of Surrey and will hopefully encourage them to make more discoveries about its food, drink, culture and idyllic countryside. Until next time, start as you mean to go on, and get stuck in to the mouth-watering recipes and fascinating stories within this book!

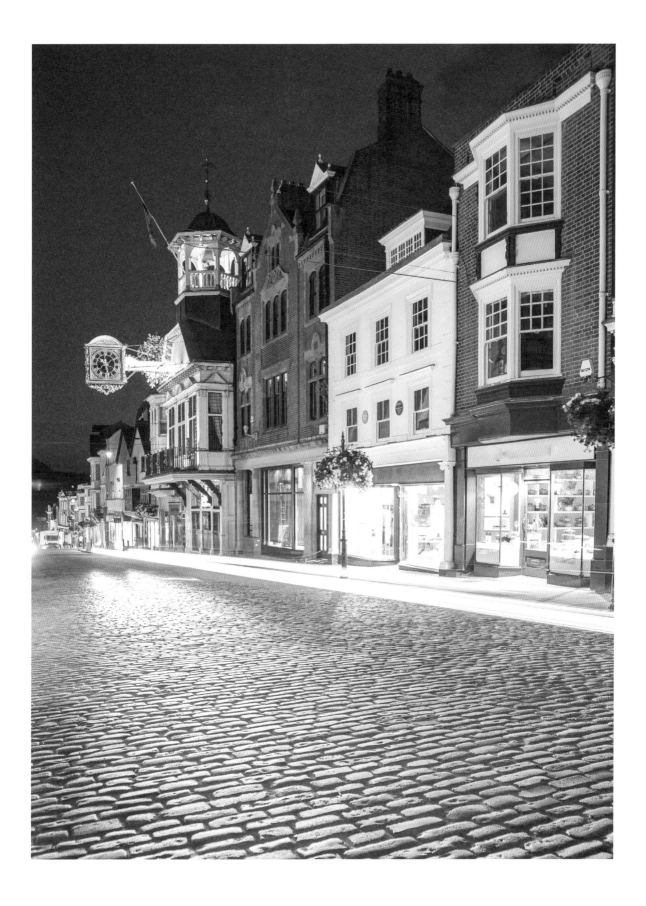

SPARKLING SUCCESS

A FAMILY-RUN VINEYARD IN THE BEAUTIFUL SURREY HILLS, ALBURY VINEYARD PRACTISES ORGANIC VITICULTURE TO PRODUCE AWARD WINNING ENGLISH WINES.

Albury Vineyard began life in 2008 when Nick Wenman, having retired from the IT industry, followed his lifelong passion for quality wine. He planted the vineyard on the southern slopes of the North Downs, an idyllic spot in the Surrey Hills, which was the perfect home for his organic approach to winemaking.

From day one, Nick believed strongly that a commitment to organic and biodynamic principles would set his wines apart from others. For Nick, organic viticulture produces better quality fruit, which of course leads to better quality wine. This passion combined with a team of excellent winemakers and a talented vineyard manager in Alex Valsecchi has led to Albury Vineyard gaining a reputation for producing the finest quality English wines.

Alex, one of the few female vineyard managers in the UK, brought her expertise to the team having attained a doctorate in Horticulture at Milan University and years of experience on vineyards in Italy and New Zealand. Her vast knowledge is crucial to the running of the vineyard, and her dogs Attila and Ulysee are much loved by visitors – in fact Attila even has a spirit named after him in the form of Attila's Bite.

Along with Alex, Assistant Vineyard Manager Dominic Travers, and winemaker Matthieu Elzinger, Nick has been joined in the business by daughter Lucy Letley, who manages the popular tours and tastings, as well as events and wine club membership. Her passion lies with making the whole vineyard as friendly and accessible as possible for guests, no matter whether they know a lot or nothing at all about wine. Granddaughter Poppy is also a regular visitor – she is most likely to be found visiting the beehives and sneaking a taste of the honey!

Albury is open to visitors for wine tastings and tours of the vineyard, or simply pop in and relax with a glass of wine on their beautiful vineyard patio, Surrey's most picturesque hidden gem. Vouchers for guided tours make an ideal gift for wine lovers, with the experience comprising a walk across scenic terrain to the top of the vineyard followed by a return to the patio to sample the latest releases. The vines are the traditional varieties of Chardonnay, Pinot Noir and Pinot Meunier, as well as some Seyval and Pinot that Nick planted for his wife, Linda. Wines include their flagship still rosé and some stunning sparkling wines, most of which have won coveted international awards.

Albury's first wine, Silent Pool Rosé was served on the Royal Barge to celebrate the Queen's Diamond Jubilee - so it certainly has the highest stamp of approval! As well as the wines, Albury also produce honey from their own beehives, some of which is made into mead. The vineyard is conveniently located next to Silent Pool Distillery and the two producers have collaborated on several spirits including a brandy and, most recently, a rosso vermouth - perfect for cocktails.

ASPARAGUS, GOAT'S CHEESE AND WALNUT SALAD

John Mobbs from Great British Wine has taken the Albury Estate Blanc de Blancs
and paired it with a simple asparagus, goat's cheese and walnut salad.

1 bunch of asparagus

A handful of walnuts

1 tbsp lemon juice, plus some
grated zest to garnish

1 tbsp olive oil

Goat's cheese

Black pepper

TO MAKE THE SALAD:

Blanch the asparagus for 1-2 minutes (depending on thickness), then remove, dry and place under the grill for 5 minutes. Meanwhile, toast the walnuts lightly in a pan and set aside.

Mix the lemon juice and olive oil together and add a twist of black pepper. Divide the asparagus between two plates and crumble over the goat's cheese. Add the toasted walnuts and dress with the olive oil and lemon juice. To finish, add a light grating of lemon zest.

ABOUT THE PAIRING:

Albury's Blanc de Blancs is a blend of Chardonnay and Seyval Blanc, the latter being a grape that I find pairs particularly well with goat's cheese. So for this pairing, I opted for a simple dish that makes the most of delicious English asparagus, with light touches of walnut, goat's cheese and lemon. The wine's crisp, intense citrus fruit and crunchy green apple freshness sits very nicely alongside the sometimes-tricky-to-pair asparagus, while the light, honeyed pastry notes complement both the goat's cheese and the toasted walnuts. A very successful pairing that respects the purity of the flavours in both the wine and the food.

Preparation time: 10 minutes | Cooking time: 7 minutes | Serves 2

SECRETS OF BREAD

AFTER YEARS AS A CHEF AND BAKER, JACK STURGESS DECIDED TO DEMYSTIFY THE ART OF BAKING BREAD, BY TEACHING PEOPLE TO MAKE PERFECT LOAVES IN THEIR OWN HOMES... AND BAKE WITH JACK WAS BORN.

When professional chef Jack Sturgess began Bake with Jack in 2013, he had no idea this unique idea would evolve into a concept that would include him appearing on Channel 4's Sunday Brunch, running a popular YouTube channel and appearing on food festival stages across the country.

When Jack first began Bake with Jack, the idea was to teach people to bake bread in their own homes, using their own ovens and their own equipment. The reasoning behind this is what Bake with Jack is all about – Jack wanted to give people the skills they need to bake bread, not simply walk them through a recipe.

"If you can build a good understanding of the bread making process itself, you can literally take it in any direction you like. You have so much freedom to experiment, and continue to learn, taking things into your own hands," he explains. "That understanding will allow you to adapt the process to fit it in and around all the things you need to do in your busy life, instead of fitting your life in around the bread!"

Although he's passionate about real bread, his home classes are about so much more than the bread itself. He loves the social aspect of getting to know people in their own homes, and the hours spent chatting and learning together. While the dough is proving and baking there is also time for Jack to share his chef skills by whipping up a medley of other delicious treats to complement the finished bread. People are always amazed by the final meal that they have made together by the time the bread is ready.

Over the last seven years, Bake with Jack has evolved to include masterclasses and training courses, as well as demonstrations in front of packed crowds on food festival stages across the country. He has a popular blog and YouTube channel, and is also a proud ambassador for the Real Bread Campaign.

"People seem to be becoming more aware of what they're eating," he says. "What we think of as 'modern' mass-produced bread with all of its additives is becoming old-fashioned. Real food is becoming popular again, and rightly so. What's more real, what's more satisfying, and what's more delicious than the loaf you've made with just flour, water, salt and yeast?"

APRICOT, SUNFLOWER SEED AND YOGHURT BATARD

This bread is essentially a savoury dough, with the sweetness coming from the fruit and nuttiness from the seeds. It's delicious to have as hot buttered toast for breakfast and equally would be perfectly in place with a baked Camembert or as part of a cheeseboard.

FOR THE DOUGH

200ml room temperature water

12g fresh yeast or 7g dry yeast

150g Greek yoghurt

15g olive oil

375g strong white bread flour

125g wholemeal flour

8g salt

FOR THE FILLING

150g sliced dried apricots

75g sunflower seeds, plus extra for topping

FOR THE DOUGH

In a mixing bowl whisk together the water, yeast, yoghurt and oil until the yeast has dissolved. Add both flours and salt. Mix with a dough scraper just until it just comes together. Cover with a dry cloth for 20 minutes. Turn it out and knead for 4-5 minutes with the heels of your hands, pushing the dough across the table, stretching gently and then folding it back onto itself. Take care not to tear it and resist the urge to dust it with flour. Rest it for 3 minutes while you clean your hands.

FOR THE FILLING

Dust the top of the dough with a little flour, turn it upside down and push your fingertips into it, spreading it into a circle. Sprinkle half the apricots and sunflower seeds over and spread evenly to the edges. Pat them slightly to stick them down. Lift the furthest edge of dough and fold it towards you a third of the way over the circle, then do the same with the side closest to you, folding it up and over the top of the first fold, with the edge of the dough meeting the other folded edge at the top. You now have a landscape rectangle. Turn it portrait and flatten it a little more. Sprinkle the remaining seeds and apricots over. Repeat the folds. Turn the dough over and, with cupped hands, tuck in underneath to make a ball. Place it into the bowl, smooth-side up, cover with a clean cloth and let rise for 90 minutes-2 hours.

DIVIDING AND SHAPING

Turn the dough out onto a dusted surface sticky-side up. Flatten it slightly and cut it in half. Pinching a piece of dough from the edge, lift it and fold it over the top. Press to stick it down just past the centre point. Work your way round the edge, doing the same thing and you should end up with a tight ball after 8-10 folds. Roll the ball over, smooth-side up. Repeat with the other piece. Dust both balls and rest under a clean cloth for 20 minutes. Dust the top of a dough ball, flip it sticky-side up and press it flat into a circle. Roll up the dough from the top edge towards you into a tight sausage. Pinch the seam together. With the palms of your hands, roll the dough gently to even out any bumps. Roll the ends with a little more pressure to make them pointy into a classic batard shape. Transfer to a lined baking tray. Brush both batards with water and sprinkle over extra sunflower seeds. With a serrated knife, make 7-9 diagonal cuts, 5mm deep. Cover loosely with dusted cling film and let rise for 45-60 minutes.

BAKING

Preheat the oven to 210°c/190°c fan/gas 6, place a baking tray in the bottom and boil a kettle full of water. The dough is ready to bake when it feels a little fragile, no longer bouncy and firm. Place the bread on the middle shelf and carefully pour the boiled water into the tray below. Bake for 30-40 minutes until golden. Tap the base and if the sound resonates, it's ready. Cool on a rack.

Preparation time: 3 hours plus prooving | Cooking time: 40 minutes | Makes: 2 loaves

CARE HOME KITCHEN

SET WITHIN 48 ACRES OF SURREY HILLS COUNTRYSIDE, BIRTLEY HOUSE, RUN BY EYHURST COURT LTD, IS A FAMILY-RUN NURSING HOME THAT HAS KEPT A FOCUS ON GROWING AND COOKING DELICIOUS FOOD FOR OVER 85 YEARS.

Birtley House has been owned and run by the Whalley/Driver family since it was registered in 1932. It was one of the first places to introduce the concept of a private nursing home, and the current Chairman, Simon Whalley – who has chosen the recipe overleaf – grew up in Birtley House.

The community-focussed nursing home is situated in serene formal gardens that are dissected by a network of easy-access paths and a plethora of benches to sit and take in the beautiful views.

Amongst the 8 acres of well-kept gardens is the fabulous kitchen garden, which supplies the estate with a bountiful supply of fresh produce. A further 40 acres of land comprises a lake stocked with trout, well-managed woodland and a large cider apple orchard.

The kitchen garden and orchard provide an abundance of seasonal fruits and vegetables, which are incorporated into the menus of the Birtley House kitchens. The creative weekly menu aims to make the most of the seasonal produce available, hand-picked from their own gardens or sourced wherever possible from local suppliers. The catering team like to avoid food waste, so any surplus home-grown fruit and veg are turned into a range of Birtley House preserves and chutneys. There is even a set of beehives, managed by Guildford Beekeepers, which produce Birtley House honey.

The adjacent woodland setting is the perfect place for artisans to practise crafts and offer courses such as stone-carving, wood-working and outdoor adventures. Surrounded by wildlife, lakes and stunning landscaped gardens, there is no more idyllic spot to enjoy the vast array of activities and events for residents of the home and the wider community, too.

With a range of activities and events taking place on the estate – which have included the Surrey Hills Woodfair and Sculpture Garden Exhibition – there is always something interesting happening at Birtley House; and with unrestricted visiting, residents can entertain guests by inviting them to enjoy a home-cooked lunch or sumptuous afternoon tea.

FAMILY FAVOURITE GAME PIE

This hearty pie originates from Joan Driver, the grandmother of Simon Whalley, Chairman of Birtley House Nursing Home, who, with her husband (Dr Lloyd Driver), founded the nursing home in the 1920s prior to the establishment of the company in 1932. The recipe evolved from a family cookbook dated 1915 – still in the family archives!

FOR THE FILLING

2 tbsp sunflower oil

900g mix of venison and rabbit (though these are often replaced with other game, such as pheasant, depending on what is available/in season)

2 red onions, sliced

3 cloves garlic, crushed

120g chestnut mushrooms, diced (may be replaced with chestnuts if no allergy concerns)

30g plain flour

1 orange, zested and juiced

1 tbsp redcurrant jelly

300ml chicken stock

300ml red wine

1 bay leaf

Salt and black pepper

FOR THE PASTRY

225g plain flour

Pinch of salt

80g lard

100ml hot water

1 egg, beaten, for glazing

FOR THE FILLING

Heat a tablespoon of the oil and brown the rabbit and venison in batches until well browned. Set aside. Heat the rest of the oil and cook the onions for 5 minutes until softened. Add the garlic and mushrooms, and cook for another 2-3 minutes. Stir in the flour and cook for 2 minutes. Season well with salt and pepper, and stir in the orange zest and juice, redcurrant jelly, chicken stock, red wine and bay leaf. Bring to the boil, add the meat and simmer very gently for 90 minutes to ensure the meat is tender. Leave to cool. Meanwhile, preheat the oven to 200°c/180°c fan/gas 6.

FOR THE PASTRY

Mix the flour and salt in a bowl. Melt the lard and the water together in a pan and bring to the boil, then add this to the flour mixture and bring into a ball. Knead and fold for a minute, then cover in clingfilm and leave at room temperature for 5 minutes. Your pastry is now ready to dress the pie dish.

TO ASSEMBLE AND COOK

After greasing the pie dish, roll out two-thirds of the pastry and press into the dish to line the base and sides. Spoon in the meaty mixture. Roll out the remaining pastry for the lid and place on top, sealing the edges and decorating as you wish, not forgetting to cut a steam hole in the centre. Glaze with beaten egg. Take your masterpiece to the oven and bake for 20 minutes, reduce the heat to 180°c/160°c fan/gas 4 and bake for a further 30 minutes, until the pastry is golden and has risen. Ensure your filling is piping hot before eating. Serve with a montage of veggies and your favourite potato, and enjoy.

Preparation time: 15-20 minutes | Cooking time: 1½-1¾ hours | Serves 6

WHEN LIFE
GIVES YOU
POTATOES...

A LOVE OF CRISPS WAS ALL IT TOOK TO LAUNCH PHIL AND VIV'S AWARD-WINNING COMPANY AND TURN THEIR SMALL IDEA INTO A BIG SUCCESS ACROSS SURREY AND BEYOND.

Before Brown Bag Crisps came into existence, owners Phil and Viv were in ordinary jobs with young children, and could never have imagined that their gamble with potatoes, oil and salt would become a well known and loved name in the world of honest artisan food. Phil decided that he wanted to work for himself, and since he'd always had a particular love of crisps, making the salty snacks seemed like an obvious path to follow. Viv wasn't convinced - "I thought it was a rubbish idea!" - but Phil was determined enough to give it a go. The shed was converted, fryers were purchased, and experiments commenced to find the perfect potato variety, type of oil and seasonings.

The next step was taking their crisps to a trade show, where they received orders from Kew Gardens and Harrods among others, and thanks to an increasing number of stockists, demand grew exponentially from there. Phil was practically living in the factory to keep up with orders, so he and Viv made the decision to close for six months, upgrade their facilities, and then continued as a hard-working team of two, juggling parenting and crisp-making with success. A price hike on olive oil caused another change of direction, but despite rebranding

and switching to sunflower oil, Brown Bag Crisps didn't lose a single customer. Viv puts this down to the personal approach they take to running the business — parents and siblings have all pitched in with everything from answering phones to frying potatoes — as well as the quality of ingredients they source to put great flavours at the forefront.

Their four initial varieties — including Lightly Salted which has won two gold stars at the Great Taste Awards — were soon joined by Oak Smoked Chilli, Tiger Prawn with Chilli and Lime, then Rosemary and Sea Salt, which are all gluten-free and packaged in the eponymous and recyclable brown bag. This innovation combined with a flair for flavour has got Brown Bag Crisps into outlets all over the UK and exported to more than ten countries, mainly through word of mouth and happy tastebuds! The team all live and work in Shepperton, where they have close ties with The Red Lion, Quality Fruit — both stockists, of course — and Willow Bakery, sharing a community spirit. Phil and Viv's next venture is a range of healthier snacks alongside the indulgent crisps, and they are looking forward to continuing to do what they love and growing Brown Bag Crisps even further in future.

CRISPY CHICKEN

This is a simple lunch or supper which can be made in minutes, yet tastes fabulous!
It's very versatile (not to mention forgiving) and could easily be adapted for vegetarians
or pescatarians by using Quorn or salmon. It's also gluten-free.

6 chicken breasts (or mini fillets
if preferred)

150g Brown Bag Oak Smoked Chilli
Crisps (use Lightly Salted or any other
flavour if preferred)

150g cheddar cheese

A sprinkle of parsley (optional)

Salt and pepper

1 egg

Preheat the oven to 200°c. Place your Brown Bag Crisps into a reusable bag or pestle and mortar and crush until they resemble breadcrumbs. Transfer to a large bowl.

Grate the cheese and mix in well with the crisps. Add the parsley (if using) and season the mixture with salt and pepper. Crack the egg into a second bowl and lightly whisk with a fork.

Dip your chicken breast into the beaten egg and then into the crispy coating until the chicken is fully covered. Place the chicken into an ovenproof dish and then repeat the process with each chicken breast or fillet until they are all coated. Sprinkle the remaining mixture onto the chicken.

Cook for 25 to 30 minutes (for chicken breasts) or 15 to 20 minutes (for mini fillets) in the preheated oven until the chicken is cooked through and crispy on top.

Serve with fresh green salad leaves (we love Quality Fruit's seasonal leaves) and a hunk of warm sourdough from Willow Bakery.

Preparation time: 5 minutes | Cooking time: 20-25 minutes | Serves 6

DRINKS WITH A TWIST

FROM KRAZY KORDIALS TO KREATIVE KOCKTAILS... BUBBLE N TWIST ALCHEMY SERVICES IS A LOCAL DRINK AND BAR SERVICE WITH A UNIQUE TWIST.

Bubble n Twist was dreamed up by Dean Hart and it all started with a single house party. Dean – who had many years of experience in the hospitality industry behind him – wanted to create a welcome drink for guests that was a little bit different to the usual offerings. Something to wow the guests and get them talking. He tapped into his experience from both front and back of house, mixed it up with plenty of research into the drinks market, added a good splash of out-of-the-box thinking and created a range of syrups that can add a twist to a variety of drink options... Hello, Twisted Syrups!

Twisted Syrups are 'kordials' that combine fruits, herbs, spices and even vegetables in ways that leave people saying, "Really? In a drink?" We're talking pea and mint (great with a G&T), raspberry and basil (perfect in prosecco) or even the incredible Thai-spiced syrup. Twisted Syrups add a twist to anything from sparkling water to G&T, vodka or prosecco. Dean has even added them to cakes. They are all hand-made in small batches using natural ingredients that are sourced locally where possible.

From Twisted Syrups, Dean moved on to create a service that offers people drinks and bar packages containing locally sourced drinks from places such as Albury Vineyard, Distillers of Surrey and Hogs Back Brewery. His hand-made bar is constructed from reclaimed scaffold boards and his drinks are served in compostable cups with paper straws. He brings 20 years of experience and knowledge to every event, to make sure he creates the perfect drinks package for the occasion.

Bubble n Twist is now becoming known for 'kocktails', too. From classic drinks to some weird and wacky combinations, Dean is passionate about mixology. He even offers kocktail masterclasses for people to mix up their own creations at home.

Twisted Syrups can now be from enjoyed at their own family-run tea shop in Shere, where you can sample 'krazy kombos' and partake in regularly held kocktail events, as well as bought in local independent shops throughout the county and you can also buy Dean's 'kombinations' online – and he is offering a return bottle policy, too. As Bubble n Twist continues to grow, they are also starting to pop up around Surrey showcasing a medley of deliciously different creations... think 'Kordial with a Twist', locally roasted coffee and homemade treats.

TURKISH XPRESSOTINI

Created in 1983 by Dick Bradsell at the Soho Brasserie in London for a customer who'd asked for a drink to "wake her up, and f**k her up". Dean has given this true classic a BnT Twist.

50ml coffee liqueur (I recommend Mr Blacks)

100ml vodka

50ml fresh espresso

25ml Turkish Delight Twisted Syrup

6 coffee beans, to decorate

Ice

Add the coffee liqueur, vodka, espresso and Turkish Delight Twisted Syrup with some ice to a cocktail shaker and shake hard until condensation appears on the shaker. Strain into chilled martini glasses and decorate the top of each drink with three coffee beans. Sit back and enjoy.

Preparation time: 5 minutes | Serves 2

BRITISH ROOTS WITH

FRENCH FLAIR

AWARD-WINNING RESTAURANT CHEZ VOUS COMBINES A LOYAL LOCAL FOLLOWING IN WARLINGHAM WITH GUESTS WHO TRAVEL FROM FAR AND WIDE TO ENJOY DESTINATION DINING.

Chez Vous opened its doors in 2011, building on a decade of success as a catering company. Having catered for thousands of events since Chez Vous Events was born in 2000, Martin Bradley joined forces with Laurent Pacaud to give Chez Vous a permanent home in Warlingham.

The building underwent a complete refurbishment to create the perfect environment for their relaxed, contemporary restaurant. They spent months choosing brilliant colours, the perfect window dressings, elegant furniture and getting the flooring and paintwork just right – and the restaurant with rooms quickly came together for its launch party in September 2011.

Between them, Laurent and Martin combine French heritage with strong British roots. Laurent started his career in France, worked under Michelin star chef Yves Chopelin in Germany and then became Head Chef of the renowned La Barbe for 27 years, before he and Martin opened Chez Vous Restaurant in 2011. With over 30 years' experience, Martin's expertise were fine-tuned in the kitchens of The Savoy, Hilton Park Lane and Gleneagles. Martin started Chez Vous Events 20 years ago, catering for prestigious weddings, parties and corporate functions all over the South East.

Chefs and proprietors, they thrive on innovation, bringing together traditional cooking and modern trends in the kitchen of Chez Vous. This fusion of classic and contemporary French cooking styles see them preparing dishes that take inspiration from all over the Mediterranean using the finest, freshest ingredients – and seasonal where possible. The menus are varied and creative, from the impressive à la carte to the special offer lunches.

Chez Vous has celebrated a string of accolades over the years. It achieved Restaurant of the Year 2016 and Hotel of the Year 2017 from Les Routiers, a Muddy Stilettos award for best restaurant in Surrey 2016, Certificate of Excellence 2019 from Hardens, and boasts a TripAdvisor certificate of excellence, as well as regularly featuring in the TripAdvisor Hall of Fame.

Thanks to its consistently accomplished cooking, relaxed atmosphere and varied menu options, Chez Vous has built an extremely loyal following within the pretty village of Warlingham over the last 8 years. As its reputation continues to reach further and further afield, it has also become an extremely popular 'destination restaurant', attracting guests from across the UK who come to stay in its beautifully refurbished rooms and sample its award-winning food.

RED MULLET, CITRUS AND FENNEL SALAD

*Light and refreshing, this citrusy salad features delicate fillets of red mullet. It is
simple and quick to prepare, but makes an impressive summer dish.*

2 oranges

2 lemons

*2 red mullets, filleted, scaled
and pin-boned*

50ml white wine, warmed

50ml extra-virgin olive oil

100g crispy mixed leaf salad

1 bulb of fennel, shredded

Salt and pepper

Preheat the oven to 180°c. Grate the zest of an orange and a lemon into a small
roasting tray. Place the 4 red mullet fillets on top of the zest and pour the warmed
white wine on top. Cook in the preheated oven for 3 minutes, then place in the
fridge to cool down.

Segment the zested orange and lemon and set aside.

Squeeze the juice from the remaining orange and lemon into a bowl. Whisk in the
olive oil and season with salt and pepper.

Place the salad, two-thirds of the orange and lemon segments, and the shredded
fennel into a bowl. Season with the citrus dressing. Place a handful of the mix on
each plate and top with a red mullet fillet cut lengthways. Drizzle the remaining
dressing over the fillet and around the salad. Decorate with the remaining segments
and serve.

Preparation time: 20 minutes | Cooking time: 3 minutes | Serves 4

COOKIES
WITH A
CONSCIENCE

A UNIQUE COFFEE BAR SERVING UP A DELICIOUS ARRAY OF HOME-BAKED TREATS, THE COOKIE BAR IS A SURREY HILLS CAFÉ WITH A BIG DIFFERENCE…

The Cookie Bar has been running as a social enterprise business since it opened in 2011. It started life with the aim of supporting Stepping Stones School in Hindhead, which caters for children with special educational needs. Managers Debbie Seagrove and Alison Johnson opened the café with the help of COINS Foundation, with 100% of the profits going back to the school.

The café would not only invest its profits back into the school, but it would provide work experience for the students in all areas of running a business. So when you sit down in The Cookie Bar to enjoy a cup of locally roasted coffee and a home-baked cookie, there will be a team of students with a range of disabilities baking, serving and operating the tills.

Not only does it give students practical work experience, but it helps them gain social skills and independence, which encourages them on their journeys to become social and economic contributors. The vibrant café with its bright red tables is a positive and uplifting environment for both students and customers. A play area and outdoor seating makes it the perfect spot for a sunny day, too.

As a social enterprise, they aim to keep costs to a minimum and to engage with the local community. With these factors in mind, the business is run with the support of volunteers. They are always looking for extra pairs of hands to volunteer supporting the students, baking cookies and serving customers.

Based in Hindhead on the edge of the Surrey Hills, The Cookie Bar makes the most of its beautiful location by serving coffee roasted in the local area, as well as fine teas, cold drinks, shakes and, of course, their home-baked cookies. They also offer a menu of light lunches and tea time bites, sandwiches to eat in or take away, and delicious homemade cakes.

Not content with running a bustling café, in 2015 they converted a 1963 Routemaster Bus into a mobile Cookie Bar, which allows them to carry their story to a wider audience. With the bus visiting festivals, fetes and other events around Surrey, The Cookie Bar team continue to create change further afield than Hindhead… inspiring people to think differently and moving towards a fairer society.

RICH CHEESE SCONES

*Savoury scones are a lunch time winner and are great with a bowl of soup. They
are made with a tasty mature Cheddar cheese, with an extra sprinkling on top.*

400g plain flour

6 level tsp baking powder

½ tsp salt

100g butter

200g mature Cheddar cheese, grated,
plus extra for topping

Milk, to mix

Beaten egg or milk, to glaze

Preheat the oven to 220°c. Line a baking tray with baking paper.

In a medium-sized mixing bowl, sift the flour, baking powder and salt. Add the
butter and rub in until it resembles fine breadcrumbs. Add the grated cheese and
stir in.

Make a well in the middle, then gradually mix in enough milk to give a soft dough.

Turn out onto a floured board, knead lightly, then roll out to 2cm thickness.

Using a 7cm pastry cutter, cut into 8 rounds and put on the lined baking tray. Brush
each one with beaten egg or milk and sprinkle some extra grated cheese on top.

Bake near the top of the hot oven for 12-15 minutes. Check halfway through baking
and turn the tray. To check if the scones are baked, tap the base of one; if it sounds
hollow then the scones are baked. Remove from oven and allow to cool.

Preparation time: 20 minutes | Cooking time: 12-15 minutes | Serves 8

WHITE CHOCOLATE AND RASPBERRY COOKIE DOUGH

Chunks of creamy white chocolate contrast beautifully with the sweet raspberries in every bite of these mouth-watering cookies.

125g unsalted butter (at room temperature)

160g caster sugar

140g light brown sugar

2 eggs

1 tsp vanilla extract

350g self-raising flour

½ level tsp salt

½ level tsp baking powder

125g white chocolate chunks

75g frozen raspberries

In a mixing bowl, cream together the butter with the caster and light brown sugars.

Gradually beat in the eggs and vanilla extract, adding a tablespoon of flour with the egg to stop the mixture curdling. Sift in the flour, baking powder and salt, and mix well. Add the chocolate chunks.

It is best to chill the dough for approx. 2 hours before adding the raspberries. Wrap the dough in clingfilm and place in the fridge to chill.

Preheat the oven to 170°c/150°c fan/gas 4. Line a baking tray with greaseproof baking paper.

Remove the dough from the fridge. Using a rolling pin, roll the dough into a 25 x 15cm rectangle. Dot the frozen raspberries over the dough, then roll together from the longest edge into a sausage shape.

The best results for these cookies are when the dough is cooked from frozen, so if you have time, you can freeze the dough at this stage. However, if you can't wait that long, cut the dough into approx. 1.5cm slices and place on the lined baking tray.

Bake in the preheated oven for 10-12 minutes if cooking from chilled (or if cooking from frozen, bake for 12-14 minutes). Allow to cool on the baking sheet for 5 minutes and then transfer to a rack to cool completely.

Preparation time: 20 minutes | Cooking time: 12-15 minutes | Serves 8

USE YOUR LOAF

FIGHTING FOOD WASTE WHILE CREATING UNIQUE BEERS – CRUMBS BREWING TAKES LEFTOVER ARTISAN BREAD AND TURNS IT INTO DELICIOUSLY DIFFERENT BEER.

Crumbs Brewing was founded by Reigate locals Morgan and Elaine Arnell in 2017 in collaboration with Chalk Hills Bakery, whose lovingly crafted artisan loaves would become the basis for lovingly crafted artisan beers.

There are two main advantages for using leftover bread to make beer. Firstly, addressing the issue of food waste is really important (did you know that 44% of bread produced in the UK goes to waste?), but secondly, the incredible taste of the bread really does lend itself to some truly delicious beers. Once Morgan started researching, he discovered that it wasn't a new idea at all – bread and beer have been intrinsically linked for thousands of years.

After months of development, using the skills of the team at Goddards Brewery to work out some of the complexities of brewing with bread, Crumbs launched their first brew in June 2017 – the Bloomin' Amber Lager. Brewed using Surrey Bloomer loaves, it's smooth and easy-drinking, with the bread contributing a rich maltiness that pleases lager and ale drinkers alike.

Crumbs Brewing spent the rest of 2017 popping up at food festivals and being featured in local media – their bready brew had become the talk of Reigate. A successful crowdfunding campaign followed, which allowed them to expand their enterprise to create two more brews: the light and zesty Sourdough Pale and the dark and mysterious Rye Ruby.

November 2018 saw Crumbs extend the idea of repurposing even further. Crumbs Rye Coffee Porter not only uses unsold Rye Bread, but also uses leftover coffee grounds from the bakery café in the brew. The rich chocolatey flavours of the coffee worked so well with the spices in the Rye bread that it's had rave reviews from several national beer writers. Hopefully it's a future award-winner.

The four beers are wonderfully unique and cover the whole spectrum of light to dark. Each reflects the taste of the artisan bread that is used to make it, which unites them as much as it differentiates them. These are beers that have been crafted to be enjoyed, as well as reducing food waste one loaf at a time. Beer, bread differently.

HAY AND BEER-BAKED ETHERLEY FARM MUTTON AND CARROTS WITH SALSA VERDE

This recipe is from our friends at The Salt Box, who love to use Etherley Farm mutton alongside our Crumbs Amber Lager.

FOR THE MUTTON AND CARROTS

2 handfuls of clean hay

2 bottles of Crumbs Amber Lager

1 bulb garlic, halved

2 stems of celery, sliced

1 white onion, sliced

1 Shoulder of Etherley Farm mutton

6 carrots

100g butter

4 tbsp chopped fresh thyme

1 tsp Maldon sea salt

1 tsp cracked black pepper

FOR THE SALSA VERDE

1 large handful of parsley and basil

1 small handful of fennel fronds (or dill) and fresh oregano

2 cloves garlic, roughly chopped

2 tbsp capers

8 cornichons

zest of ½ lemon

4 anchovy fillets (optional)

3 tbsp cider vinegar

1 heaped tsp Dijon mustard

6-8 tbsp rapeseed oil

FOR THE MUTTON AND CARROTS

Place the hay in a roasting tin and soak in the beer. Place the garlic, celery and onion into the middle of the hay. Preheat the oven to 200°c/180°c fan/gas 6. Rub the mutton leg all over with the butter and sprinkle over the thyme, salt and pepper. Place the leg onto the tray and pull the hay around the meat. Cover with tin foil and bake for 1 hour

Reduce the oven to 160°c/140°c fan/gas 3 and continue to cook for a further 2-3 hours or until the meat becomes tender and begins to fall off the bone. Add the carrots in the final hour of cooking.

Transfer the leg to a platter to rest, discard the hay and vegetables, but keep the carrots. Split the carrots down the length and sear on a griddle pan for extra flavour.

FOR THE SALSA VERDE

Pick the leaves from the herbs, place on a chopping board with the garlic, capers, cornichons, lemon zest and anchovies. Finely chop everything together. Place the chopped mixture into a bowl and mix in the vinegar and mustard. Stir to combine and finally add the rapeseed oil.

TO FINISH

Arrange the grilled carrots on a large platter, shred large chunks of mutton on top and drizzle with the salsa verde.

Preparation time: 30 minutes | Cooking time: 4 hours | Serves: 4-6

STORIES

FROM THE SUBCONTINENT

DASTAAN IS A VIBRANT CAFÉ RESTAURANT IN EWELL, SOMETHING
OF A HIDDEN GEM WITH TWO STARS OF AUTHENTIC INDIAN CUISINE
AT ITS HEART.

The journey to Dastaan's opening in late 2016 began long before then, with the careers of its two co-owners and chefs. Nand Kishor grew up in the Himalayan foothills, and discovered a flair for cookery on moving to Mumbai which is where Sanjay Gour also got into the hotel and restaurant industry. They didn't meet there, however, but in London several years later. Both chefs built distinguished reputations for themselves, working for the likes of Angela Hartnett and JKS Restaurants – the company behind Trishna and then Gymkhana where they did finally meet in 2013.

Sanjay and Nand just 'clicked' and both of them enjoyed working in a relaxed yet disciplined atmosphere with plenty of good-humoured banter in the kitchen. After a while the two of them began discussions about extending their friendship into a business partnership and opening a new restaurant in their own right. Financing the venture was the biggest problem, but they made the decisions to set up Dastaan out of town, and Sanjay's wife had enough faith in the venture to re-mortgage their house and take out a loan: quite some vote of confidence!

Everyone's hard work and commitment paid off, and Dastaan is now an extremely lively, bustling and friendly place. The front of house staff are efficient and well-informed, keeping on top of things in the cosy restaurant and serving two sittings a night which are almost always full. Sanjay and Nand serve totally authentic Indian food, prepared from the finest fresh ingredients. Each dish is individually made with a light and modern touch, and exquisitely presented. They have avoided the plated style of food employed in some high-end restaurants because they believe one of the fundamentally important aspects of true Indian food is that it is to be shared.

Nand's culinary approach is strictly rooted in authenticity while Sanjay's experiences of modern European cuisine and the sophistication of French pastry and desserts add outstanding refinement to the menus. Chaat, kebabs, tikka, curries and meetha (Indian sweets) represent diverse areas of Indian food, paired with a Mumbai café style interior that pops with as many bright colours as the dishes. Both chefs are really happy with what they have achieved through ambition, vision, sheer dedication, and plenty of honest hard graft. Between them, they have created a truly unique experience for diners to enjoy.

DASTAAN दास्तान IS AN URDU WORD
IT MEANS **STORY**, FABLE, TALE
IN HINDI **KAHANI** / कहानी
NEETIKATHA / नीतिकथा, KATHA / कथा
FOR EXAMPLE "HAMARI DASTAAN
KHANE KE ZUBANI" WHICH MEANS
**OUR FOOD WILL TELL
YOU OUR STORY** .....

Dastaan
INDIAN RESTAURANT

© 020 8786 8999
W Dastaan.co.uk
Dastaan 447

SPICED LAMB CHOPS

This recipe stems from chef Nand Kishor's roots in Northern India. It's a classic way to marinate meat and cook in a tandoor or on a grill. He has elevated and refined this dish into a firm favourite among his guests at Dastaan.

1kg French trimmed rack of lamb

Pinch of chaat masala (Indian spice blend)

FOR THE GINGER AND GARLIC PASTE

30g ginger, peeled and grated

30g garlic, peeled and grated

100ml cold water

4 tbsp vegetable oil

FOR THE FIRST MARINADE

4cm ginger (unpeeled)

45g ginger and garlic paste

10g ground kasuri methi (fenugreek)

7.5g salt

40g Kashmiri chilli powder

25ml lemon juice

45ml mustard oil

FOR THE SECOND MARINADE

300g Greek yoghurt

2 green chillies, finely chopped

15g ginger and garlic paste

7.5g turmeric

5g ground kasuri methi (fenugreek)

10g Kashmiri chilli powder

15g garam masala

First, slice the lamb rack into 3 to 4cm ribs. Cut down between every two ribs starting from the smaller end, to leave a chop with just one bone at the larger end of the rack. Carefully cut away one bone from each of the first three chops, then carefully pound each chop with a meat mallet. A rack of seven ribs should give you four fat chops.

FOR THE GINGER AND GARLIC PASTE

Blend the ginger and garlic with the water and oil to create a smooth paste. This will make slightly more than you need for the marinades.

FOR THE FIRST MARINADE

Mix all the ingredients together and apply the marinade to the prepared lamb chops. When the meat is well coated, lay the chops into a container in one layer and then leave to marinate in the fridge for a minimum of 12 hours and up to 36 hours.

FOR THE SECOND MARINADE

Combine the ingredients and once again rub the paste well into the lamb chops. Leave them to marinate in the fridge for up to another 12 hours.

Thread the cutlets onto skewers, passing them two or three times through each piece to secure the meat well. In the restaurant, we cook the lamb chops in the tandoor for 5 to 6 minutes at 220°c until they are nicely charred. The best way to replicate this at home is to cook the chops in an oven preheated to 180-185°c for about 10 to 12 minutes.

Sprinkle the lamb chops with a little chaat masala before serving them with freshly made coriander and mint chutney and some sliced onions.

Preparation time: 2-3 days | Cooking time: 10-12 minutes | Serves: 4

SPECIALITY BUTCHERS

FROM THE HEART OF DORKING TOWN CENTRE, THE DORKING BUTCHERY
ARE BRINGING AGE-OLD TRADITIONS BACK TO THE HIGH STREET.

Despite being open for just four years, The Dorking Butchery has already acquired a string of accolades, including Best New Butchery Business at the Butchers Shop of the Year Awards in 2016 and Butcher of the Year at the Surrey Life Food & Drink Awards in 2017 and 2018. With awards for Outstanding Customer Service to boot, it's clear that their traditional approach to service rivals their passion for sustainable, organic and free-range meats.

The Dorking Butchery was founded in 2016 by two young butchers, Alex Emmett and Gary Core. They have worked tirelessly since the shop opened to build a business that balances the traditions of butchery with a cool, contemporary edge. Gleaming white tiles are the backdrop for the young, dynamic team – donned in white shirts, grey aprons and flat caps – to chat with customers.

"It's important for us to understand what people really want," says Alex, "sometimes the array of meat cuts can be quite intimidating and so we always spend time with our customers and give them advice about what might work best for the recipe they're planning."

They specialise in dry-aged beef, maturing it for 4-6 weeks to ensure maximum tenderness and flavour. In fact they hold a prestigious Great Taste Award for their signature classic burger, made to a secret recipe from rare-breed dry-aged beef. They will even help you select your own cut and breed of beef, and it will be aged on-site to your exact liking. Now that's personal service.

There's a strong sense of community spirit in Dorking, and the gang at The Dorking Butchery love to collaborate with and support other local businesses, including a variety of pop-up butchery demonstrations. You'll often find them "team-building…" in the Queen's Head, too. The Dorking Butchery hessian bag is becoming a symbol of the community, thanks to their environmentally friendly avoidance of plastic packaging wherever possible. You'll get your meat wrapped in paper, too, of course.

With seasonality and provenance at the heart of the business, the offerings change throughout the year. Pop in for a chat with one of the knowledgeable butchers and they can help you decide what will be perfect for your dish – whether it's a midweek meal or a dinner party show-stopper. Just don't leave without some of their homemade pork scratchings…

IN SEASON
HARE
PIGEON
CLAMS
GUINEA FOWL
VENISON
UNICORN

DRY AGEING NOW
SOUTH DEVON
HEREFORD
BRITISH WHITE
SUSSEX
SHORT HORN
LINCOLN RED

RECIPE OF THE WEEK :
PERSIAN LAMB STEW
BY THE SALT BOX

DORKING BUTCHERY
SPECIALITY BUTCHERS

FIELD TO FORK

WORKING WITH LOCAL SUPPLIERS IS AT THE VERY HEART OF THE DORKING BUTCHERY, SO FINDING FARMERS WHO SHARE THE SAME PASSION FOR SUSTAINABLY PRODUCED FREE-RANGE AND ORGANIC MEAT HAS ALWAYS BEEN VITAL.

Nestled in the heart of the Surrey countryside Etherley farm produces high welfare lamb, chicken and duck. Their slow grown free-range chickens are left to roam and forage naturally surrounded by ancient woodland, undulating fields and unspoiled meadows. At the foot of Leith Hill, only a stone's throw away from the Butchery, this local farm resides within the Surrey Hills, designated as an Area of Outstanding Natural Beauty.

Just over the border in Sussex, Will Sheffield and his family follow traditional farming methods and practise age-old techniques passed down through the generations. Their organic farm, Clayton Farm, which is situated in Mayfield, is approved by the Soil Association. Alex and Gary love to visit this farm to see the animals living naturally in small herds and families. Their turkeys are famous at Christmas time, and they can be ordered from The Dorking Butchery. Other meats available from Clayton farm include beef and pork.

Finally, a bit closer to home, in fact just down the road in Ockley, Kevin and Nikki Pinnegar produce old fashioned Gloucester old spot pork, it is one of only a few true pure breeding lines left in the country. Truly free-range and left to forage naturally, its clear to Alex and Gary that higher welfare animals really do produce better quality products. Roasting joints, sausages and bacon are made from the wonderful pigs at the Butchery and feature throughout the year.

THE DORKING BUTCHERY'S

GUIDE TO STEAK

IF YOU'RE THINKING OF BUYING A LOVELY LOCAL STEAK TO COOK AT HOME, LET US SHOW YOU HOW TO ACHIEVE STEAK PERFECTION WHATEVER CUT YOU CHOOSE.

OUR GOLDEN RULES TO THE PERFECT STEAK

- Source high quality ingredients as better quality meat is worth every penny.
- Always ensure your steaks are brought to room temperature before cooking.
- To season your steaks, we recommend coarse sea salt flakes and ground black pepper.
- Invest in a thick, heavy-bottomed pan, skillet, griddle or barbecue.
- The leaner the cut, the less cooking time your steak will require.
- Fat is flavour – the more marbling, the more succulent your steak will be.
- Steaks on the bone such as T-bone and côte de boeuf can be finished off in the oven.
- Always allow resting time, as your steak will continue to cook after removed from the heat.
- Cuts such as bavette will benefit from being cut against the grain.

STEAK ACCOMPANIMENTS

PEPPERCORN SAUCE

2 tbsp mixed peppercorns • 60g butter • 1 finely diced shallot • 100ml brandy • 100ml beef stock • 60ml double cream

Gently crush the peppercorns in a pestle and mortar. In a saucepan, melt the butter. Add the shallots and sauté on a medium heat until soft, then add the peppercorns and brandy, allow to simmer for 3 minutes. Add the beef stock, simmer for a further 3 minutes, then finally add the cream, reducing the heat to low. Heat through, then season with salt to taste.

BEARNAISE SAUCE

250g butter • 1 shallot • 1 tsp peppercorns • 1 bay leaf • 2 sprigs tarragon • 2 tbsp white wine vinegar • 2 egg yolks • 1 tbsp lemon juice • 2 tbsp chopped tarragon

Finely dice the shallot and lightly fry in a touch of oil. Remove from the heat and allow to cool slightly, then add peppercorns, bay leaf, tarragon stalks and vinegar. Bring to the boil, then remove from heat, strain and set aside. Melt the butter in the pan. Bring another small pan of water to a simmer, then whisk egg yolks in a heat proof bowl with the flavoured vinegar above the simmering pan of water. Whisk until it begins to thicken, then slowly add the melted butter. Finally, stir through the lemon juice and fresh tarragon.

CUTS AND COOKING INSTRUCTIONS

BAVETTE
Rich, beefy and open-textured.
Sear on high heat for 3 mins each side. Slice against the grain.

CÔTE DE BOEUF
Robust, succulent and full of flavour.
Char the marbling until crispy. Finish quickly in a hot oven.

FILLET
Soft, lean and tender. Best served rare.
Cook quickly for 2-3 mins each side on a high heat.

FLAT-IRON
Full of flavour and cooks quickly. Best served rare.
Flash fry for 2-3 mins each side on a fierce heat.

SIRLOIN
Classic, tender and tasty.
Cook for 2-3 mins each side. Serve medium-rare.
Rest after cooking.

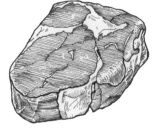

RIB-EYE
Well marbled, tender and full-flavoured.
Cook on the hottest heat for 3-4 mins each side. Crisping the
fat is the secret to a good rib eye.

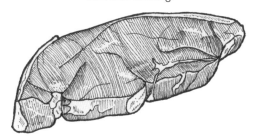

RUMP
Affordable and versatile.
Cook for 4 mins each side. Best served medium rare.
Rest after cooking.

T-BONE
Added flavour from cooking on the bone.
Cook on gentle heat for 4-5 mins each side.
Resting time is essential.

Cooking times will vary from cut to cut and will depend on the thickness of your steak.
Chat to our team of friendly butchers about what's best for your steak.

Illustrations by Andy Cockell

FLAT IRON STEAK WITH ROCKET AND PARMESAN

*Quick, easy and tasty, this Dorking Butchery staple is a perfect mid-week meal.
The key is to allow the meat to rest before slicing, so that the middle of the steak
is just blushing but warm throughout.*

600-700g flat iron steak
500g rocket
Good-quality Balsamic vinegar, to taste
Good-quality extra-virgin olive oil, to taste
Parmesan cheese, to taste
1 handful of sweet balsamic baby onions
Salt and black pepper

Start by seasoning the flat iron steak with salt and pepper. We recommend cooking the steak in one piece and slicing after. For best results, sear the steak on a high heat for approximately 3-4 minutes on each side. When the steak has what looks like a nice heavy crust on the outside, remove from the heat and place on a cutting board to rest and slice later.

Dress the rocket leaves with olive oil and balsamic vinegar and arrange on a plate. Grate or shave over enough Parmesan for your taste; we find the salty Parmesan goes perfectly with sweet, sharp balsamic vinegar, so tend to use a lot.

Return to the steak after a few minutes resting and slice into thin bite-size strips. Place on top of or next to the rocket salad and scatter over and around the sweet baby onions.

To accompany the steak, try serving with thick-cut chips or griddled cherry tomatoes, and serve with a glass of full-bodied red wine.

Preparation time: 15 minutes | Cooking time: 5 minutes | Serves 2

LAMB CUTLETS, SPRING VEGETABLES AND SALSA VERDE

LAMB CUTLETS, SPRING VEGETABLES AND SALSA VERDE

This lovely spring recipe is vibrant and flavourful, making the most of locally farmed lamb. We have used 3 cutlets per serving, but you can do more if you like.

6 lamb cutlets

Spring vegetables (whatever is seasonal – we used radishes, Tenderstem broccoli and baby carrots)

Salt and black pepper

FOR THE SALSA VERDE

Small bunch of fresh mint

Small bunch of fresh basil

Large handful of fresh flat leaf parsley

8 tbsp extra-virgin olive oil

3 tbsp red wine vinegar

2 tbsp anchovy paste

1 tbsp Dijon mustard

1 lemon, juiced

Small handful of capers

First make the salsa verde. Roughly chop the mint, basil and flat leaf parsley and set to one side. In a mixing bowl, combine the olive oil, red wine vinegar, anchovy paste, Dijon mustard and lemon juice, and gently whisk together. Add the olive oil mixture to the chopped herbs and pour in the capers. Give it all a good mix together and set aside. Your salsa verde dressing is done.

Place a pan of salted cold water on to boil; we will come back to this when it has reached a fast boil.

Next season the lamb cutlets with salt and pepper and grill or griddle for 3-4 minutes on each side – you are looking for a golden brown colouring all over and the fat to be crispy.

Back to the pan of boiling water. Plunge the baby carrots and Tenderstem broccoli into the boiling water and allow to simmer away for a few minutes. Meanwhile, slice the radishes into small discs.

Drain the veg and arrange on the plate. Scatter the radishes over the spring veg and place the lamb cutlets on top. Drizzle the salsa verde over and enjoy with a nice chilled glass of rosé.

Preparation time: 20 minutes | Cooking time: 10 minutes | Serves 2

PAN-SEARED GLOUCESTER OLD SPOT PORK CHOP WITH ROASTED FENNEL AND CHERRY TOMATOES

You could use any pork chops for this, but the Old Spot breed in particular carries a little more fat, making it perfect for crispy crackling. This recipe works really well on a barbecue.

2 Gloucester Old Spot pork chops

2 large fennel bulbs

2 large shallots, peeled

150g drained cooked cannellini beans

2 handfuls of sweet cherry tomatoes

1 handful of fresh basil

Salt and black pepper

Olive oil, for drizzling

Chargrilled lemon wedges, to serve

Preheat the oven to 200°c/180°c fan/gas 6. Season the pork chops with salt and pepper.

The pork chops will take the longest to cook so start by searing on a hot griddle pan or barbecue. You'll need to sear for 5-6 minutes on each side and then transfer to the oven to cook all the way through. A thick chop will take approximately 15-20 minutes to cook through. Alternatively you can move to a cooler part of the barbecue and allow the heat to gently rise through it.

Next, cut the fennel and shallots into four pieces. Cook them as you did the pork and sear until they start to show colour – this will be perfect on the barbecue (if using) or a griddle pan. Allow the fennel and shallots to turn golden brown. As they start to cook through, the fennel will start to break down and become soft and silky. Transfer to a mixing bowl, add the cannellini beans and drizzle with a little olive oil.

Place the cherry tomatoes onto the griddle and allow the skin to blister until the juices run out. Combine this into the bowl with the fennel. Tear up the basil and fold through the veg.

Serve with the seared pork chops and char-grilled lemons for a delicious summery feast.

Preparation time: 10 minutes | Cooking time: 30 minutes | Serves 2

A PERFECT PAIRING

LOCAL PRODUCE AND MATCHES MADE IN HEAVEN ARE ALWAYS THE ORDER OF THE DAY FOR THE DRUNKEN MOUSE, A SURREY CATERING COMPANY WHICH – AS ITS NAME SUGGESTS – PUTS WINE AND CHEESE CENTRE STAGE.

Kathryn and Sam, the duo behind The Drunken Mouse, are as passionate (if not more so) about delicious wine and mouth-wateringly-good cheese as the French. It's this infatuation with the perfect pairing that gave them the edge to follow through with their passion and open their own Surrey-based street food and catering business.

The couple have always had a passion for sourcing cheese and drinks that go fantastically together. Sam is a sommelier and the son of a cider maker, while Kathryn's first job was on a cheese counter and she has been food blogging since 2012 (check out www.homemadewithmess.co.uk for some of her recipes).

After putting together a charity event in 2017, where the most popular area was a cheese and wine bar, they realised that this was their calling and launched The Drunken Mouse in 2018. From their very own 'Methuselah' – a converted 1960s horsebox – The Drunken Mouse rattle out some of the very best cheesy flavours at festivals and private events, with the added benefit of a liquid accompaniment! They always aim to bring the best locally sourced produce to their customers and move around to suit the needs of any event.

The Drunken Mouse supper clubs and cheese and wine tasting events also offer something different to the norm, with flavours, textures and pairings at the forefront of these culinary experiences. If you can't wait to get to one of these events, they can also come to your own venue to offer bespoke catering experiences.

The couple are passionate about the best quality local produce and do their utmost to share in the food experiences they create and enjoy. Living in the South East, they are lucky enough to be surrounded by some of the best cheese in the UK, which challenge French camembert and even Dutch gouda. There's no shortage of top notch drinks either, including home-grown sparkling wines from Albury Vineyard and others, along with charismatic local gins from Silent Pool and renowned beers.

The Drunken Mouse is now filling up the event calendar for next year and putting together some exciting and unusual supper clubs that will be popping up around Surrey. Keep an eye out online and on Instagram for some exciting announcements about collaborations with other local businesses, preparing for boozy, cheese-filled evenings at only the best local venues.

SAUSAGE & STICKY CIDER ONION TOASTIE

*Pork & cider, a match made in heaven! Now throw in some crusty sourdough and
oozing, smoky cheese and you have yourself the ultimate toasted sandwich!*

FOR THE CIDER ONIONS

*2 large red onions, peeled and finely
chopped*

30g butter

200ml dry cider

1 tbsp soft brown sugar

1 tbsp cider vinegar

Salt and pepper

FOR THE SANDWICH

*250g good quality sausage meat (we use
GJ Honours in Old Woking)*

5 tsp wholegrain mustard

1 tbsp oil, for frying

*80g smoked cheese (we use Smoked
Duddleswell from High Weald Dairy)*

*150g strong cheddar (we use Sussex
Charmer)*

80g mozzarella

*8 slices of sourdough bread (we used a
delicious loaf from Bake with Jack)*

50g butter, softened

To make your sticky cider onions, heat the butter in a saucepan and fry the onions for 5 minutes, until soft. Add the remaining ingredients to the pan, give it a good stir and leave to simmer away, stirring regularly, until all the liquid has been absorbed and the onions are lovely and sticky. This could take 30 to 40 minutes.

Once cooked, mix half the onions with the sausage meat and one teaspoon of the mustard, then shape into four flat patties. Heat the oil in a frying pan and fry the patties for a few minutes on each side until golden and crispy.

Preheat your oven to 180°c and heat a large griddle or frying pan. Grate your cheeses and mix it all together.

Butter your bread and lay the slices out so the buttered sides are on the board. For each sandwich, spread one teaspoon of the mustard on one slice and a spoonful of the onions on the other. Crumble a sausage patty onto each slice of bread that has the onions and then divide up the cheese on top of that. Complete each sandwich with the mustard slice of bread.

Fry your sandwich on the hot griddle or pan for 2 minutes on each side and then pop on a tray and into the oven for 5 minutes to ensure that the cheese is gooey in the middle and the bread lovely and crispy on the outside.

Slice in half and tuck in with a refreshing glass of cider!

Preparation time: 45 minutes | Cooking time: 10 minutes | Serves: 4

LOCALLY GINSPIRED

FROM THE SURREY HILLS, ELSTEAD VILLAGE DISTILLERS HAVE BEGUN PRODUCING A SELECTION OF SMALL-BATCH GINS FROM 500-YEAR-OLD THUNDRY FARM.

Elstead Village Distillers was founded in 2017 by Paul Shubrook and Neil Redit, bringing together many years of friendship and a shared passion for gin.

Neil had moved into the cottage on the 500-year-old Thundry Farm owned by Paul and his wife Christine. Neil and Paul attended a gin experience at the City of London Distillers, where they made their first gin and got their first taste of small-batch distilling. Everyone who tasted their gin was impressed and, after sampling many more gins at a London Gin Festival, Paul and Neil decided that theirs really did pass muster.

August 2017 saw them launch their brand Thundry Hills Gin – following a last-minute branding change after a trade-mark dispute led them to change from their original name of Surrey Hills Gin. By February 2018 all the licensing was in place and Thundry Hills Gins were being produced in two 40-litre stills – around 50 bottles at a time.

Elsetad Village Distillers puts small-batch production at its core. Everything is done on the farm, from distilling and bottling to labelling and branding. Every label details the batch and bottle number. They hand-deliver bottles across the county, although it is also available to order online – and you'll see bottles appearing in pubs as far away as York.

The first two gins are based on their original recipes. Thundry Hills Original was Paul's recipe. It's rich-tasting and smooth, with hints of sweet orange peel. It is perfect for enjoying neat, but it also lends itself to cocktails, such as those overleaf. Thundry Hills Sanctuary is Neil's recipe, named after the bird sanctuary Thundry Hills Meadow just across the road. It's a traditional gin that is best enjoyed with a plain tonic.

A further two gins have since been added to the collection. A fruity offering, Thundry Hills P.M. is distilled with pears and mangoes. Unlike commercial fruit gins, no fruit juice is added to the gin – it is all distilled in one go, giving it a crystal clear finish. A fourth gin, Thundry Hills Michaelmas, is a seasonal gin that is based on winter spices. It was very popular last Christmas and is sure to be returning this year.

ELSTEAD GIN COCKTAILS

Two delectable cocktail recipes that star Thundry Hills Original Gin.

FOR THE ST. PATRICK'S DAY GIN COCKTAIL

12.5ml crème de melons

25ml Thundry Hills Original Gin

50ml Indian tonic

3 cubes of ice, to serve

Frozen melon ball, to serve

2 bruised mint leaves, to serve

FOR THE THUNDRY HILLS ORANGE COCKTAIL

12.5ml cointreau

25ml Thundry Hills Original Gin

50ml Indian tonic

3 cubes of ice, to serve

Orange slice, to serve

FOR THE ST. PATRICK'S DAY GIN COCKTAIL

Mix the Crème De Melons, Thundry Hills Original Gin and tonic in a glass with ice. Add the frozen melon ball and bruised mint leaves, and serve.

FOR THE THUNDRY HILLS ORANGE COCKTAIL

Mix the Cointreau, Thundry Hills Original Gin and tonic in a glass with ice. Add the orange slice and serve.

THUNDRY HILLS GIN SORBET

This Thundry Hills sorbet is an essential on a hot summers day. Present in a Thundry Hills Gin glass and garnish with a thin slice of lime. Choose which gin to use and pair the fruit accordingly. Cheers!

240ml water (we recommend a good quality chlorine-free bottled filtered water)

65g granulated sugar

600ml tonic water

120ml Thundry Hills Gin of choice

FOR P.M. THUNDRY HILLS GIN SORBET

1 lime, zested and juiced

½ mango, crushed

FOR ORIGINAL THUNDRY HILLS GIN SORBET

1 large sweet orange, zested and juiced

For Sanctuary Thundry Hills Gin sorbet:

2 limes, zested and juiced

First, make a simple syrup. Heat the water and sugar in a saucepan on the hob, making sure the sugar has all dissolved. Turn off the heat and add the zest and juice from the fruit of choice – depending on which gin you are going to use. Allow it to cool.

Once cooled, add the tonic water and gin. (if you want more gin and less tonic, then adjust the tonic to gin ratios accordingly, but don't overdo the gin as it may not freeze properly).

Strain through a sieve. Pour the strained liquid into the bowl of an ice cream machine and follow the machine's instructions for freezing a sorbet. If you don't have an ice cream maker, place the finished sorbet in the freezer, take it out after 30 minutes and liquefy in a food processor, then freeze again. Repeat the last step until you have the correct consistency. This is time-consuming, but by doing this a few times you will prevent large ice crystals from forming and you'll end up with a smooth sorbet.

Keep frozen, you may want to take it out a several minutes before serving to allow it to soften a little.

Preparation time: 5 minutes each | Each serves 1

Preparation time: 30 minutes, plus freezing | Makes 1 litre

GRAPE TO GLASS

FROM ITS UNIQUE GEOGRAPHY TO ITS STATE-OF-THE-ART WINERY, GREYFRIARS VINEYARD IS THE IDEAL SPOT TO PRODUCE (AND ENJOY) SOME OF ENGLAND'S FINEST SPARKLING WINES.

There has been a vineyard at Greyfriars for over 30 years. Around 1,500 vines were planted in 1989 on a one-acre site situated on the south-facing slopes of the Hog's Back at Puttenham, only a ten-minute drive from nearby Guildford and Farnham in the beautiful Surrey Hills. When its current owners Mike and Hilary Wagstaff took over in 2010, they had ambitions to turn this hobby-scale vineyard into a boutique commercial winery.

Brother-in-law David Line came on board as vineyard manager and the new family business set to work planting vines until they had a 40-acre vineyard. The grapes predominantly comprise the classical Champagne varieties of Chardonnay, Pinot Noir and Pinot Meunier, but they also have small plots of Pinot Gris and Sauvignon Blanc, too.

They released their first wines in 2013 from the 2011 vintage, and have received a plethora of international wine awards, including a Gold Medal and the coveted English Sparkling Rose Trophy from the International Wine Challenge 2019 for their Sparkling Rose Reserve. So, what is it that makes Greyfriars wines so good? "It's partly down to the location," explains Mike, "the chalky soil combined with the sunlight on the south-facing slopes of the Hog's Back make this perfect wine-growing country."

It is also a stunning place to work and to visit. The vineyard has a Cellar Door Shop and tasting room that is open all year round where there is always wine open to taste and one of the small, friendly team on hand to welcome you and introduce you to the vineyard. With views across the North Downs – almost as far as the sea – Greyfriars Vineyard is a glorious place to visit. They run tours and tastings throughout the spring and summer where people can get to know the story of Greyfriars Vineyard, meet the family behind the business and see the place where the wine comes from. "People like to drink a story," explains Mike, "they want to know the provenance of their wine, just like they do their food." The vineyard also runs seasonal Open Day events that are free of charge to attend and a range of other exciting events all year round.

Their mission is to persuade British people to drink more English wine and it seems to be working – the vineyard has gone from producing 2 tonnes of grapes to 200 tonnes in 2018. They now make in the region of 100,000 bottles of wine a year, with a wide range of sparkling and still wines on offer.

In addition to the Cellar Door Shop and tasting room, the wines are also available to buy directly from Greyfriars' online store and an increasing number of retail outlets – from farmer's markets and farm shops to Michelin-star restaurants, and even iconic venues such as the Champagne Bar at St Pancras Station and the Crypt Tearoom at St Paul's Cathedral.

GUAZZETTO DI MERLUZZO

This recipe has been kindly provided by Fulvio, Nicky and the team at Olivo Restaurant, a lovely family-owned Italian restaurant in the heart of Guildford town centre (www.olivo.co.uk). It is paired with Greyfriars Sparkling Cuvée Royale, a food-friendly sparkling wine that works perfectly with the fresh flavours of the fish.

1 beef tomato
1kg fresh cod fillets
20g capers
60g pitted black olives
600g white potatoes
12 large king prawns
50ml extra virgin olive oil
2 garlic cloves, whole
300ml fish stock
300ml fresh tomato sauce
Chopped parsley
Salt and pepper

FOR THE RECIPE

Skin and deseed the beef tomato. Cut the cod fillets into smaller pieces (5-6cm). Thoroughly rinse the capers and halve the black olives. Peel the potatoes, cut into medium-sized cubes and boil in salted water until just cooked. Drain and cool. Peel the prawns, using the discarded shells to make your own fish stock if preferred.

Add the oil to a large, wide frying pan and place on medium heat. Add the whole garlic cloves, olives, capers and the chopped beef tomato. Fry gently, removing the garlic once golden brown. Add the fish stock, bring to a rolling simmer, then add the tomato sauce and continue to cook for a few minutes until slightly reduced.

Place the cod fillets evenly in the pan so that they are all covered and leave to cook through. Add the potatoes and finally the king prawns, gently moving the pan in a circular motion to cover evenly with the sauce. Cook for a few minutes until the prawns have cooked through. Finally, add the parsley and season with salt and pepper to taste. (You may also wish to drizzle a drop of chilli oil if you like a little heat.) Serve in a large flat pan or plate with a choice of toasted sourdough or ciabatta. Buon appetito!

ABOUT THE PAIRING

Greyfriars Sparkling Cuvée Royale is the first exceptional limited-edition release from our best vineyard site. Citrus and red apple notes are balanced by a round, elegant palate that offers a lovely hint of biscuit on the finish. We made only 2400 bottles of this wine and each are individually numbered – it's a special one.

Vintage 2015
Vineyard The grapes came from our 2011 planting at Greyfriars.
Grape varieties 50% Chardonnay, 50% Pinot Noir.
ABV 12%.
Winemaking The grapes were hand-picked and whole bunch-pressed. Fermented and aged in old oak barrels. Put through malolactic fermentation.
Bottled May 2016.
Numbers 2,400 bottles.
Disgorged March 2018 onwards.
Released May 2018. This wine has had a minimum of 24 months on the lees and cork.
Price £30.00 a bottle
Available At Greyfriars Vineyard Cellar Door Shop and online at www.greyfriarsvineyard.co.uk.

FROM INDIA WITH LOVE

FOR AUTHENTIC INDIAN FOOD MADE WITH FRESH PRODUCE, MANDIRA'S KITCHEN IS SURREY'S ONE-STOP SHOP FOR DELICIOUS READY MEALS, CATERING, SUPPER CLUBS AND MORE, INSPIRED BY ONE WOMAN'S JOURNEY FROM EAST TO WEST...

Mandira grew up on a tea plantation in Assam: an "idyllic childhood" during which she experienced Indian food in all its shades and hues. However, when she later moved to the UK with her husband after also living in Calcutta for a time Mandira discovered that, contrary to people's expectations, she couldn't really cook. Indian food in the UK is very different to the regional cuisines she was used to, so she had to learn quickly in order to reclaim those flavours because "the best food comes out of the family home."

When her work in management consultancy came to a sudden stop, Mandira made a decision to pursue her newfound skill and her love for home-style dishes that carried a personal history with them. A trip back to India in 2016 provided the perfect opportunity for culinary exploration, and shortly afterwards Mandira hosted her first supper club for family, friends and food lovers with local influence. It was a real success and the business, simply and aptly named Mandira's Kitchen, then went from strength to strength.

There is now a dedicated manufacturing kitchen and event space on site – right next to Silent Pool Gin, with whom Mandira has recently collaborated to create an Orange and Gin Chutney – to provide customers and stockists with freshly prepared food, blast-chilled to preserve all the goodness and then frozen to be sold in farm shops all over the county, or bought online and shipped by overnight courier to any UK address. The venture still hosts supper clubs as well as offering cookery classes, and caters for events as varied as weddings, formal dinners for hundreds of people, anniversary celebrations for couples and more.

The team make sure everything is made with love to produce food that defies typical expectations of Indian ready meals. Nothing is oily or greasy and not all contain chillies, because each creation has a story and comes from indigenous regional dishes that aren't formulaic or Anglicised. This commitment to quality and real flavour has brought Mandira's Kitchen recognition and a well-established place within the community, including accolades for innovation in retail, Great Taste stars and Product of the Year in the 2019 Surrey Life awards. The business always has something new up its sleeve, and Mandira is keen to continue developing her ideas and passion for offering home-style food.

KOLAPATA MAACH
FISH IN BANANA LEAVES

No proper wedding in Calcutta is complete without these morsels of deliciousness. The fish is smothered in a mixture of coconut, coriander and mustard, wrapped in banana leaves and then steamed or baked. A huge family favourite, these have become ever so popular at our catered events.

Any firm white fish fillet, as fresh as you can manage to find

5 pieces of banana leaf (each about the size of an A4 sheet of paper)

FOR THE MARINADE

4 tbsp freshly grated coconut (frozen or unsweetened desiccated coconut will work too)

½ a bunch of fresh coriander leaves

1 or 2 green chillies (depending on how hot you want it)

1 tsp English mustard powder

¼ tsp salt

2 tbsp oil

½ a lemon, juiced

Cut the fish fillet into five thick 5cm by 7.5cm pieces. If you cannot find banana leaves for this recipe, then just use tinfoil.

FOR THE MARINADE

Blend all the ingredients together into a paste. If you are using desiccated coconut, you may need to add a little water to the mixture. The marinade needs to be a thick paste and not runny at all. Taste it to make sure it has enough salt and if you need it hotter, add more green chillies.

Gently rub the marinade into the fish, then cover and set aside for 30 minutes or so.

To prepare the banana leaves, wipe them with a damp tissue and then one by one, carefully wave them over an open flame (ideally on a gas hob) so that they are gently scorched. This makes them easy to wrap without cracking. Now lay them flat on a table.

Lay a piece of fish in the centre of each banana leaf (or piece of tinfoil) with some extra marinade. Now gently fold the leaf over the fish, like you are wrapping a parcel, and securing each one with a toothpick. Lay the parcels on a greased baking tray.

Preheat your oven to 180°c and bake for 20 minutes until the banana leaves are brown. Serve the fish with steamed rice.

Preparation time: 10 minutes, plus 1 hour marinating | Cooking time: 20 minutes | Serves: 5

A HOME FROM HOME

MISS POLLY CAFÉ IS THE NEW PLACE TO EAT IN MOLESEY, HAVING BEEN ESTABLISHED IN 2017 AND GROWN STEADILY WITHOUT LOSING ITS FAMILY-FRIENDLY PERSONAL TOUCH, AND OF COURSE THE MENU OF DELICIOUS HOMEMADE FOOD.

Dale and Jo had always wanted to run a café, but thought of their ambition more as a retirement dream than the next step in their careers. However, on a family visit to the UK (they were living in Australia at the time) the couple came across a café in Molesey and had a chat with the owner. Even when they flew back, the idea didn't go away, and eventually Dale and Jo decided to make a go of it by moving back and establishing their own business at the venue. Dale went first to completely renovate the café, then Jo joined him with their two young children to open Miss Polly Café in 2017.

Since that leap of faith, the new eatery has gone from strength to strength and really integrated with the Molesey community. "We pride ourselves on being a bit different," says Jo, "which I think has made people more inclined to support us because we're offering more and genuinely have a passion for making this work." Miss Polly quickly diversified by hosting supper clubs and creating a catering branch too, which provides food for all occasions and meals including barbecues, breakfast events, hot and cold lunches with a varied menu to choose from. It didn't take long for the café itself to take off either, which lead to the owners expanding into next door to double the size of their venue.

Whoever they are cooking for, Dale and Jo use top quality local ingredients to prepare their food, from proper breakfasts to light salads and hearty burgers. The café can boast coffee by Chimney Fire Coffee based in the Surrey Hills, fruit and veg from the award-winning Paull's Greengrocers in Thames Ditton, bread from Frankonia Bread House in Surbiton, meats from Bentleys Butchers of Distinction in Molesey and free-range eggs from Chapel Farm in Surrey. Talking to people and knowing what they want is really important to the enterprising owners, whether it's favourites on their everyday menu or inventive dishes for themed evening meals at the supper clubs. The food and the customer's experience are central to everything they do, and they are always striving to improve by developing the business accordingly.

That commitment paid off recently when Dale and Jo won a contract to run cafés at both Hampton Court Palace and the Tower of London; they had an incredibly busy season but relished the opportunity and look forward to spending more time at Miss Polly again to put everything they've learnt back into their own venture, making the Molesey café a wonderful place to eat for everyone.

SHAKSHUKA EGGS

This is an absolute favourite in the Miss Polly Kitchen and at home. It can be served in individual dishes or in a larger dish for a sharing plate. There are so many delicious ways to change and modify this dish to make it a winner for everyone.

3 large peppers (the more variety of colours the better)

2 large red onions

2 cloves of garlic, crushed

½ tsp cumin

1 tsp smoked paprika

2 tsp vegetable oil

400g tinned chopped tomatoes

50g tomato purée

Salt and pepper, to taste

2 eggs per person

Sourdough toast, to serve

Deseed the peppers then slice them into long strips. Peel and halve the onions and then cut them into 5mm slices. Add the oil to a heavy-based saucepan and place that on a medium-high heat.

Add the sliced peppers, onions and crushed garlic to the pan and sweat for 10 minutes, stirring regularly. Everything should soften during this process. Add the cumin and paprika then continue to cook for a further 5 minutes, stirring regularly.

Add the tinned tomatoes and tomato purée and continue to cook at a low simmer for about 30 minutes until all the ingredients are very soft and the sauce has thickened and reduced. This process can be done up to 24 hours prior to adding your eggs. The flavours in the sauce will intensify over time, so you would be best to cook this part the night before and store them in the fridge.

When you're ready to add the eggs, spoon the sauce into ceramic or glass baking dishes (you can either use individual ones or make one large dish for a great sharing breakfast). The sauce should be hot when placed in the baking dishes so will need to be reheated gently if you have prepared it the night before.

Make shallow wells in the sauce and carefully crack the eggs into those spaces, adding two eggs per person. Place the baking dishes in the centre of a preheated oven at 200°c and bake for 10 to 12 minutes for runny eggs or 12 to 15 minutes for medium-well done eggs.

Serve the shakshuka scattered with fresh micro herbs and freshly toasted sourdough for dunking.

Looking for something a bit different? This recipe can easily be spiced up. Try adding some of the following: fresh or dried chillies, Cajun pepper, fresh spinach leaves, chorizo or goat's cheese.

Preparation time: 20 minutes | Cooking time: 2 hours | Serves: 4-6

A ROARING GOOD TIME

THE RED LION HAS MASTERED THE TRICKY BALANCING ACT OF REMAINING A TRUE VILLAGE PUB WHILE OFFERING SUPERB DINING, WHERE HONEST FOOD AND DRINK TAKES CENTRE STAGE.

Owners James and Steve are Shepperton born and bred, having known each other since primary school and stayed friends over the years. They shared an interest in the old pub first and foremost, but gained widespread experience as a chef and restaurant manager respectively before migrating back to the village and taking over The Red Lion in 2014. Since then, they have transformed their former watering hole into a destination to rival the best London gastropubs with a winning combination of fantastic food and plenty of bar space for those who just want a cosy spot to sup in.

The food menus move with the seasons thanks to a plethora of local suppliers and producers alongside a commitment to making as much as possible in house, from bread to ice cream. Fruit and vegetables are sourced from a family-owned grocer in Shepperton that's going on a century old, all the meat is high quality and comes from a single butcher, and even the crisps are made nearby. "We are absolutely focused on the best of the best, because if we're going to do anything why not give it 100%?" says Steve.

Examples of this passion for quality and close attention to detail include the only deep sea mussels in the UK, searched out and included as a staple of the evening menu, and the 33 hours of preparation that goes into the brined and buttermilk-soaked chicken wings. It doesn't stop with the edibles either, as the bar is brimming with great cocktails, wines selected by a small Dorset-based company who know where to look for unusual but brilliant value bottles, and craft beers from up and down the country.

There's also The Fish Shack on Fridays that serves takeaway fish and chips, and a river garden that boasts waterside tables, its own bar, music and even boat moorings for idyllic summer days eating and drinking al fresco. Updating the pub's design has been an important part of the journey, with an open plan bar, snug and dining room created from the existing spaces and brightened up with open fires and exposed brick to give The Red Lion a truly cosy feel.

Sustainability has always been important to Steve and James too; they have recently introduced a 'carbon free dining' scheme and make sure all waste is managed properly without single use plastics. The pub is now up for the Heineken Star Pub Awards in 2020 thanks to its perfect marriage of village local and a cracking place to dine out.

SLOW-COOKED SHORT RIB AND SALT-BAKED CELERIAC

This recipe takes a shoe leather-tough piece of beef and slowly transforms it into a succulent and delicious dish. Aged on the bone, marbled, and also known as Jacobs Ladder, this is one of our favourite cuts.

8 pieces of short rib on the bone, cut between 190g-220g (ask your local butcher)

FOR THE MARINADE

700ml water

150ml light soy sauce

100ml apple juice

20ml mirin

20ml sesame oil

240g sugar

400ml good beef gravy

FOR THE SALT BAKED CELERIAC

2 large celeriac (roughly 400g each)

525g plain flour

575g salt

275ml water

8 egg whites

FOR THE MARINADE

Combine all the ingredients in a saucepan, bring to the boil, turn down and simmer for 10 minutes. Set aside.

Sear the short ribs in a frying pan with a little oil until browned all over, then transfer them to a deep tray. Cover the meat with the marinade then tightly cover the tray with one layer of baking parchment and two layers of tin foil to keep the heat locked in. Cook the beef for 16 hours at 90°c in the oven (overnight might be the best time to do this, ready for lunch or dinner the next day).

Remove the beef from the tray and place onto a chopping board or large plate. Pour the sauce into a large deep-sided frying pan, bring to the boil and then reduce to a shiny glaze. Gently pull out the bone from each of the short rib pieces and place the meat in the pan, gently turning each piece to coat it in the sauce.

FOR THE SALT BAKED CELERIAC

Wash the celeriac thoroughly, trim off any roots and slice a small slither off the base so they sit flat.

Mix the rest of the ingredients together to make a paste. Line a tray with baking parchment, put two small dollops of the salt crust down, ensuring they are wider than the celeriac base. Sit the celeriac on top and use the rest of the salt crust to completely cover them. Bake in the oven at 160°c for 2 hours 30 minutes, or until a skewer can penetrate through to the centre without resistance.

TO SERVE

A lovely sociable way of serving this for a dinner party would be to put the beef in a nice serving dish on the table with some fresh watercress on top. For the celeriac, use the heel of a knife to gently crack the salt crust, creating a lid, and place them on the table with a serving spoon. You can add any other sides of your choice, but a good horseradish is a must!

At The Red Lion we allow the celeriac to cool so we can cut a nice big cube out, then fry this in a non-stick pan with butter until golden. We also serve the beef with buttered sprout tops, crushed carrot and swede, and horseradish. We hope you enjoy this simple but delicious dish.

Preparation time: 30 minutes | Cooking time: 16 hours | Serves: 8

FUN AND
FEASTING FOR ALL

RICHMOND'S SURREY FOOD FESTIVAL OFFERS A GREAT DAY OUT AND THE OPPORTUNITY TO SAMPLE ALL KINDS OF CUISINES, FRESHLY PREPARED BY THE VERY BEST FOOD STALLS IN THE SOUTHEAST.

With its cornucopia of food styles and bottomless supply of drinks, Surrey Food Festival satisfies every palate. Want to find some tips and tricks on how to prepare such delightful dishes yourself? Visit the demonstration theatre, take a seat, and relax while learning top culinary secrets from the masters. Afterwards, take time to chat to the celebrities: sometimes you can even enjoy tasting samples of the dishes you've just seen prepared. There's always a great line up of award-winning chefs, authors of the latest cookbooks, mixologists and more.

Next, visit the Marketplace to source ingredients, appliances and latest kitchen gadgets. There are food stalls offering all manner of fare, from burgers, Thai, barbecues and pizzas to churros, ice cream and cannoli. Craft beers, artisan gins, wines and coffees are also available all day, so visitors can quench their thirst while feasting their stomachs as well as their eyes!

When your culinary curiosity is satisfied, relax in the Chill-Out Zone, or rock out at the live music stage. The main stage hosts a variety of bands and artists who perform throughout the day. Acts are curated from both the national and local music scene, and have featured performers as young as five years old. Everyone is welcome to bring rugs and spread out on the grass. It's a great way to enjoy an afternoon of music, relaxation, great food and drink.

Families don't need to worry: children are admirably catered for as well as the adults. The Kids Zone keeps them entertained and happy all day; there are rides, different inflatables offering challenges, sporty activities, face painting and much more. That just leaves one thing for you to do…relax and enjoy it all.

Surrey Food Festival is just one of several festivals brought to you by The Local Food Festival, specialising in food and drink themed events designed to cater for families. Check out the website thelocalfoodfestival.com for details of all the year's amazing days out, designed for you and your family. While you're there, join the mailing list to receive details of all the events, and be the first to receive details of special offers. Find and follow us on social media too @thelocalfoodfest.

TIME TO REWILD

INSPIRED BY FOOD AND FIRE, THE SALT BOX BRINGS PEOPLE TOGETHER IN THE GREAT OUTDOORS FOR UNFORGETTABLE FEASTS COOKED OVER FIRE IN SURREY AND THE SOUTH EAST.

A totally unique and inspiring culinary venture, The Salt Box was created by two adventure-loving foodies who share a passion for wild ingredients, local produce and the irresistibility of a crackling open fire. Beckie and Christian joined forces in 2017 – and The Salt Box was born.

Two sustainably minded cooks, Beckie and Christian put seasonality at the heart of the business. The aim was to create delicious food from the plethora of nature's humble ingredients, cooked over an open fire and enjoyed beneath the trees.

"From seasonal suppers to breakfast in the woods, lakeside picnics to afternoon tea in the trees, our feasts over fire showcase the very best of our doorstep produce, all enjoyed around our signature shared dining tables," they explain.

The shared dining experience is an important aspect of The Salt Box ethos. All of their dishes are designed for sharing, creating a convivial atmosphere between old friends and new. As well as connecting diners with each other, each feast aims to reconnect people with what's on their plates. They describe it as a "nose-to-tail and root-to-fruit ethos" – nothing is wasted and everything is celebrated.

Events range from supper clubs to cookery courses, and they have collaborated with a variety of local businesses to showcase the incredible produce available here in Surrey. "We are committed to strengthening our local food community and work closely with local farmers and artisans who harvest and produce outstanding products at the peak of their ripeness and flavour. It's fresher, hasn't had to travel far, keeping our money in the local economy – to us, it's a no-brainer," they explain.

They have created a loyal customer base already and, in 2018, just a year into business, they were awarded Surrey Life's Newcomer of the Year award, as well as the Surrey Hills Trademark.

SPICED WILD VENISON WITH WILD HERB FLATBREADS

We love to use wild and foraged ingredients, and there's an abundance of wild game meat available here in Surrey, which is not only delicious but really sustainable. This recipe is great cooked over an open fire, but equally delicious cooked in your kitchen at home!

FOR THE VENISON

6 tsp coriander seeds

6 tsp cumin seeds

2 tsp black peppercorns

6 tsp paprika

4 tsp garam masala

4 tsp garlic powder

4 tsp ground ginger

2 tsp chilli powder

1 tsp ground cinnamon

3 tsp ground turmeric

5 tbsp natural yoghurt

500g wild venison

FOR THE FLATBREADS:

300g self-raising flour

½ tsp bicarbonate of soda

1 tsp salt

1 handful of chopped fresh herbs (we use wild herbs such as wild garlic, ground ivy)

300g natural yoghurt

FOR THE VENISON

Toast the coriander seeds, cumin seeds and black peppercorns. Transfer the spices to a pestle and mortar, allow to cool. Finely grind the spices, then stir in the rest of the spices. Place 4 tablespoons of the tandoori spice mix into a large bowl and stir in the yoghurt. Place the rest of the spice mix into a jar for another day.

Cut the venison into cubes and marinate in the spice mix for at least 2 hours. Meanwhile, make the flatbreads.

FOR THE FLATBREADS

Sift the flour with the bicarbonate of soda into a large bowl. Add the salt, chopped herbs and then the yoghurt, and combine into a nice soft dough. If the dough is too sticky add a touch more flour. Leave the dough to rest for a few minutes before using.

Take the dough out of the bowl and place on a floured work surface. Divide the dough into 10 portions. Roll each piece into a ball and, using a rolling pin, roll a few millimetres thick.

Heat a large frying pan/griddle pan and dry fry your flatbreads, turning every few minutes. When they begin to puff up they're ready! Place the flatbreads onto a plate and cover with a tea towel until serving so that they don't dry out.

TO FINISH

Skewer the cubed venison and grill on high heat for 10-12 minutes turning frequently. Allow the venison to rest for 5 minutes before serving. Serve the venison and flatbreads on a large serving board so everyone can dig in and help themselves!

Preparation time: 40 minutes, plus 2 hours marinating | Cooking time: 20 minutes | Serves 4

THE
SECRETT'S OUT

WITH A FARM SHOP, ARTISAN CRAFT BEER AND GIN COLLECTION, SEASONAL PICK-YOUR-OWN, BUTCHER, ENGLISH WINE MERCHANT, TEA SHOP AND ETHICAL CLOTHING STORE ALL ON SITE AT SECRETTS AWARD-WINNING FAMILY FARM, IT'S NOT JUST A PLACE TO SOURCE DELICIOUS LOCAL FOOD AND DRINK BUT A WELCOMING DESTINATION FOR GREAT DAYS OUT.

Greg, the current managing director of Secretts, is proud to be following in the footsteps of a long line of family members who have kept this farm going since 1908, when his great-grandfather began to work the land. As London grew, the venture moved outwards and settled in Milford around 30 years later. That same 150 acres is where the Secretts business stands today, having started to diversify in the '70s and transformed the old stable blocks into its first farm shop.

With such experience behind them, the farm has stayed very similar in terms of produce: the bulk of the work is still done by hand and new varieties are chosen for flavour over yield to ensure everything remains the best possible quality. Best known for salads and root vegetables of all colours and sizes, Secretts grows something for every season including brassicas, sweetcorn, asparagus and huge fields of soft fruits for the well-established pick-your-own.

All this fresh produce goes into the farm shop, where it is sold alongside a wide range of deli goods from cheese and crackers to wine, beer and gin. Freshly baked breads, a free-from section and zero-waste dispensers can also be found in the farm shop while the cold counter makes the most of home-grown ingredients. Sweet and savoury bakes such as pies and quiches usually star the bumper crop of the season, and are ready to take home or out into the grounds for a picnic: there's plenty of open space for walking dogs and enjoying the outdoors on the farm.

If that wasn't quite enough to fill your day out with fun, Eliza's Tearoom serves breakfast and lunch alongside cakes and scones, just in case the weather proves too temperamental! The cake bakers took over in 2015 with a passion for great home-style cooking. There's an ethical clothing and gift store, Jo's Jumpers, as well as an English wine merchant on site too, and to complete a perfect Sunday roast the award-winning Black Barn Butchers is the place to go.

It's no wonder that Secretts has scooped Surrey's Best Farm Shop from Muddy Stilettos and come runner up in the Surrey Life awards three years running! The farm is a well-loved part of the local area, proven by the huge numbers of people who attend the pumpkin and sweetcorn festivals held annually, getting pickers into the fields and celebrating the crops with plenty of food and fun.

VIBRANT VEGETABLE WELLINGTON

This is a dish that we love to cook when we fancy a break from meat. It's colourful, delicious and made using gorgeous vegetables fresh from our fields. It tastes great enjoyed as a roast dinner or with a side salad for a lighter meal.

500g butternut squash, cut into 1cm cubes

2 tbsp olive oil

Small bunch of sage, chopped

Salt and pepper

2 onions, chopped

500g mushrooms, sliced

3 cloves of garlic, crushed

150g cooked chestnuts

1 nutmeg, for grating

500g puff pastry

1 egg, beaten

6-8 cooked beetroot

Sesame or poppy seeds

Heat the oven to 200°c. Toss the squash with half the oil, half the sage and some seasoning. Tip onto a baking tray and roast for 25 minutes in the oven until tender.

Meanwhile, heat the remaining oil in a large frying pan and fry the onion for 10 minutes until tender. Add the mushrooms and fry for 15 minutes until softened, and the liquid has evaporated. Add the garlic and remaining sage to the mushrooms. Fold in the chestnuts and roast squash. Season everything well, adding a grating of nutmeg. Leave the filling to cool before assembling the wellington.

Roll the pastry out on a floured work surface to a 35 by 45cm rectangle. Transfer to a large parchment-lined baking sheet with one of the long sides of the pastry facing towards you. Spoon the mushroom and squash mixture down the length of the pastry, leaving a 7cm border along the top and 1cm on both sides. Brush all the exposed pastry with beaten egg.

Put the beetroots in a line down the middle of the filling; they should be touching. Fold the filling-covered, long length of the pastry over the beets, using the paper to help you. Roll up and trim the pastry with a knife when it's overlapping by 1cm.

Place the wellington seal-side down, and pinch the ends to seal them. Egg wash the whole thing and use a fork or blunt cutlery knife to score the pastry in a pretty pattern. Chill the wellington for at least 30 minutes, or up to 24 hours.

Heat the oven to 200°c again. Brush the chilled wellington with more beaten egg, sprinkle with the sesame or poppy seeds and bake for 45 to 50 minutes until golden brown and puffed up. Leave to rest for 10 minutes before carving into chunky slices with a sharp knife to serve with your choice of a lovely fresh salad or all the trimmings of a roast!

Preparation time: approx. 1 hour, plus at least 30 minutes chilling | Cooking time: 1 hour 20 minutes | Serves: 8

STILL WATERS RUN DEEP

NAMED AFTER A TRANQUIL SPOT IN THE SURREY HILLS AMIDST THE ROLLING COUNTRYSIDE OF THE ALBURY ESTATE, THIS UNIQUE DISTILLERY DRAWS INSPIRATION AND INGREDIENTS FROM THE LAND AROUND IT TO CREATE AWARD-WINNING GINS AND MORE.

Silent Pool Distillers has creativity at its core, along with a natural chalk-filtered water source from its beautiful rural location. Founders Ian and James came across the Silent Pool on the Duke of Northumberland's Albury Estate, and knew they had discovered the perfect spot to turn their vision for an independently-owned, handcrafted gin distillery into reality. A vintage steam-fired boiler was restored to power the handmade copper still and, following a nine-month development period that included 650 different distillations, Silent Pool Gin was born.

This award-winning contemporary London Dry gin is handcrafted with 24 botanicals and water from the Silent Pool using a unique four-stage process that layers an intricate balance of classic, floral and citrus notes. Silent Pool Gin's beautiful bottle features a botanical design that has since been transformed into a range of gifts, and is known throughout the county as an iconic representation of the gin's natural origins. The on-site shop, tours, and regular events like tasting days held at the distillery allow the team to share this story and really engage with their customers, establishing the venture as part of the landscape much like its well-loved namesake.

It's not just the flagship gin that keeps people coming back for more, as the distillers love to let their creative juices flow by experimenting with seasonal botanicals to produce small batches of locally inspired spirits, including gin cordials and vodka. Whether it's sweet and spiced redcurrants in autumn or fresh greengages in winter, there's always something new to look out for.

This innovation doesn't stop at spirits, either, as the distillers were the first to introduce liquid garnishes to enhance your G&T – a spritz of extra flavour designed to marry with the flavours in Silent Pool Gin. They also use local honey, not for sweetness but for smoothness and texture. "We pride ourselves on producing something that's accessible but complex, and give our distillers a canvas to paint on when it comes to exploring new product ideas," says head marketer Darren.

Silent Pool Distillers now exports to 35 countries worldwide as well as selling its spirits online, at the distillery shop and at local farmers' markets and events. Despite this growth, every part of the production process – from weighing out the botanicals to distillation and bottling – is still carried out by the team of distillers at the small distillery on the banks of the Silent Pool.

These cocktails are inspired by our rural home in The Surrey Hills. Our honey comes from beehives that neighbour the distillery, and blackberries grow in abundance in the local hedgerows.

THE SILENT POOL GIN BEES KNEES

The sweetness of honey is cut through with fresh lemon in a delicious cocktail that is beautifully balanced by our award-winning gin.

50ml Silent Pool Gin

20ml honey (if the honey is set then warm it slightly to soften it)

20ml freshly squeezed lemon juice

Ice

In a cocktail shaker, stir the gin and honey together until the honey has dissolved. Add the lemon juice and then fill the shaker with ice. Shake and strain into a chilled cocktail coupe or martini glass. Garnish with tart redcurrants or a twist of lemon peel.

THE SILENT POOL GIN BRAMBLE

The perfect cocktail for late summer foragers: you can flavour this fruity cocktail with freshly picked wild blackberries.

6 freshly picked blackberries, plus 1 for garnish

50ml Silent Pool Gin

20ml lemon juice

20ml sugar syrup

Ice

Muddle the blackberries in the bottom of the glass then add the gin, lemon juice, sugar syrup and ice so that the glass is two thirds full. Mix with a long-handled spoon, top with ice and garnish with a blackberry to serve.

Preparation time: 5 minutes | Serves: 1

SEASONED TO TASTE

WELL SEASONED KITCHEN IS A BUSINESS RUN BY CHEF GEMMA TAYLOR BRADSHAW, WHICH CENTRES ON HER LOVE OF SEASONAL AND LOCAL FOOD, INCLUDING PRODUCE GROWN ON HER OWN ALLOTMENT, AND HER COMMITMENT TO SUSTAINABILITY.

Cooking had always been a passion for Gemma, but it wasn't until she followed her love of the outdoors to the French Alps that it became her livelihood, and eventually evolved into the business that she owns today. "I come from a family where food is really important," she explains, "but actually fell into the industry because I wanted to work in the mountains and got into chalet catering, then spent the best part of ten years there."

When Gemma returned to the UK, it was her husband's family allotment in Surrey that was the catalyst for her new venture. "When I started to cook back home, seasonality was just becoming big news for chefs, but I felt quite disconnected at first because I didn't know much about British produce." Growing her own fruit and vegetables was the antidote, and encouraged Gemma to become a regular market stall holder. Creating an outlet for what her allotment produced became the inspiration for her food, and over the next five years Well Seasoned Kitchen developed organically – literally and figuratively – to incorporate catering and collaborations for events and pop-ups across the region. Today Gemma runs the business full-time alongside being a mum to two children. She has recently focussed on production to supply farm shops around Surrey.

She describes her approach as 'veg-centric', making the most of what she grows and forages, while staying connected to a love of the outdoors. Wild garlic in spring, hedgerow fruit in autumn, nettles and dandelions can all be found in her nearby woodlands around Woking and the Surrey Hills. This makes Well Seasoned a more sustainable business which has been a priority for Gemma since the beginning; she is currently reducing plastics in the packaging of her food and is always evaluating transport and storage options to make her processes more environmentally friendly.

Gemma is still a regular at Ripley Farmers' Market, where she sells quiches, savoury bakes and pastries, soups and stews, and enjoys being part of the local community along with lots of other growers and makers, shaping her business around Surrey's evolving food and drink scene. "The food scene in Surrey is really thriving, with businesses and projects springing up in communities throughout. It's great that I can be part of that in ways that work with my approach to seasonal, sustainable cooking."

Well Seasoned Kitchen

- Lentil & tomato Ragu (vegan)   £4.50
- Leek & Jerusalem Artichoke
                    Soup (vegetarian)
- Squash, coconut & Coriander
                    Soup (vegan)   £3
Quiches   £3
- Smoked Bacon & Kale
  Caramelised Onion, Herb

Herby Sausage
Rolls.   £2.50
Contains Mustard, Milk, Gluten

WELL SEASONED KITCHEN
LENTIL & TOMATO RAGU

WATERCRESS AND BLUE CHEESE TART WITH SEASONAL SLAW

This tart uses locally grown watercress from Kingfisher Farm Shop. It's a delicious ingredient all year round which pairs beautifully with a mellow blue cheese, such as Brighton Blue from High Weald Dairy. A variety of seasonal vegetables can be used for a bright slaw with the sweet lemon dressing.

FOR THE PASTRY

100g cold butter

200g plain flour

3 tbsp whole milk

FOR THE TART FILLING

2 large bunches of watercress

1 tbsp rapeseed oil

100g mild blue cheese

4 large eggs

2 tbsp crème fraiche

140ml whole milk

½ tsp salt

FOR THE SEASONAL SLAW

400g seasonal vegetables (such as carrots, red or white cabbage and celeriac – you could also use fennel, sprouts, radishes, beets, apple and red onion)

FOR THE SWEET LEMON DRESSING

1 tbsp mild honey

1 tsp Dijon mustard

½ large lemon, juiced

1 tbsp apple cider vinegar

90ml cold pressed rapeseed oil

This recipe makes 1 large tart (22cm tin) or 4 small tartlets (10cm tin). Preheat the oven to 200°c.

FOR THE PASTRY

Cut the cold butter into small pieces, add it to the flour and rub in until the mixture resembles breadcrumbs. This can also be done using a food processor. Add the milk a little at a time until the pastry comes together in a ball, then knead a little until smooth. Roll out the pastry on a lightly floured surface to 5mm thick then line the tart tin or tins. Cut away any excess around the edges before placing the pastry in the fridge while you prepare the filling.

FOR THE TART FILLING

Thoroughly wash the watercress, chop the stems into 2cm pieces and roughly chop the leaves. In a pan, heat the rapeseed oil and gently sauté the stems for 2 minutes, then add the leaves and sauté for a further 2 minutes. Roughly chop the blue cheese into 2cm cubes and set aside. In a bowl, whisk together the eggs, crème fraiche, milk and salt.

Line the chilled pastry case with baking paper and fill with baking beans or dried pulses, then place in the preheated oven for 8 to 10 minutes until lightly golden. Remove the beans and lining then turn the oven down to 175°c. Place the pastry case in its tin on a baking tray before filling with the wilted watercress and pieces of cheese. Pour over the egg mixture to fill the case. Place the tart in the oven for 20 to 30 minutes until lightly set and golden. Allow to cool a little before serving.

FOR THE SEASONAL SLAW

While the tart is cooking, prepare the slaw and dressing. Peel and grate the carrot, thinly slice the cabbage and any similar vegetables, and julienne the celeriac into matchsticks.

FOR THE SWEET LEMON DRESSING

Combine the ingredients for the dressing and whisk well. This will keep in a jam jar in the fridge for a week. Just before serving, combine the prepared slaw with a generous amount of the dressing.

TO SERVE

Serve the tart warm or at room temperature with a side of seasonal slaw and some fresh watercress to garnish.

Preparation time: 40 minutes | Cooking time: 30-40 minutes | Serves: 4 — makes 1 large tart (22cm tin) or 4 small tartlets (10cm tin)

A WELL-SPICED

HIDDEN GEM

FAMED FOR ITS MODERN YET RELAXED GOLFING ETHOS, THE WISLEY IS NOW BECOMING KNOWN FOR EXTENDING THIS APPROACH TO ITS DINING OPTIONS...

Just outside of Ripley, and nestled behind the RHS Wisley Gardens, is The Wisley, a private members golf club. The Wisley boasts 27 holes of impeccably conditioned golf, in three loops of nine holes all returning to the striking Lutyens-inspired Clubhouse, as well as world-class practice facilities that make the club a true haven for golfers.

In recent years, The Wisley has extended its famed modern yet relaxed ethos of golf towards its food and beverage operation. Under the guidance of Head Chef Sam Peschier, the club is now also a culinary destination for members looking to enjoy a relaxed yet refined meal in exceptional surroundings.

The recently refurbished Clubroom is the hub of the club and provides an elegant modern bar and restaurant reminiscent of the finest London hotels. Crescent-shaped, with a terrace that overlooks the impeccable golf course, it's the perfect environment to frame a round of golf with excellent refreshments.

With an effortless attention to detail, exceptional standards of service and the nurturing of a uniquely warm atmosphere, The Wisley boasts a food experience unlike any other golf club. The menu, which changes seasonally, is built on the provenance of ingredients and inspired by the diversity of the international membership. Signature dishes range from Traditional Breakfast and the staple Club Sandwich, to Pad Thai (The Wisley's bestseller for the last three years), and Red Thai Curry, adapted for the recipe overleaf.

As well as managing the requirements of the internationally diverse members, the menu caters for The Wisley's numerous tour professionals and members for whom a healthy diet is key to their fitness and performance. It's a delicate balance relished by Sam and his experienced kitchen team, who create daily specials and unique snacks to not only complement the club menu, but also to showcase new skills and dishes that surpass expectations.

The food experience is key to The Wisley; it supports the unique atmosphere and camaraderie of the club and is central to the busy social calendar. From gastronomic tasting experiences and monthly supper clubs to family Sunday lunches or themed evenings, the underlying principle of relaxed yet refined cuisine is key to the club – and truly feeds the passion for golf.

TIGER PRAWN THAI CURRY

The stock is the key part of this recipe so take your time and reduce slowly to intensify the aromatic flavours. Serve with your choice of rice. We recommend Thai glutinous rice known as sticky rice, which is available in most supermarkets.

FOR THE PASTE

1 clove garlic

2 red chillies

25g fresh coriander including stalks

25g fresh basil including stalks

40g root ginger, peeled

1 white onion, peeled

2 tomatoes

1 tbsp red Thai curry paste (shop-bought is fine)

Vegetable oil, for cooking

FOR THE SAUCE

2 litres chicken stock

1 litre tomato juice

50g root ginger, sliced

3 sticks lemongrass, crushed

100g galangal, sliced

2 x 400ml tins coconut milk

40g palm sugar

6 lime leaves

Thai fish sauce, to taste

TO FINISH

30 large tiger prawns, butterflied

40g garlic butter

200g cherry tomatoes, halved

1 bunch spring onions, sliced

1 chilli, finely chopped (optional)

50ml double cream

25g coriander, roughly chopped

FOR THE PASTE

Blitz all the paste ingredients together in a food processor until coarse. Sauté in a pan on the stove with a little oil for 10 minutes without it colouring too much.

FOR THE SAUCE

Add the chicken stock and tomato juice to the paste and bring to the boil. Add the root ginger, lemongrass and galangal to the stock and simmer for 2-3 hours, adding extra water if needed. Simmer away and reduce the stock by half and then add the coconut milk, palm sugar and lime leaves. Reduce until thick and creamy. Add a couple of splashes of Thai fish Sauce and check the seasoning. Pass through a medium sieve and set aside.

TO FINISH

Sauté the prawns in a large pan with the garlic butter, then add in the cherry tomatoes and spring onions. If you want extra spice then add 1 chopped chilli, then pour in the Thai curry sauce and reduce down until thickened, add a dash of double cream for the extra silky finish, sprinkle with fresh coriander and serve.

Preparation time: 30 minutes | Cooking time: 3 hours | Serves 6

DIRECTORY

THESE GREAT BUSINESSES HAVE SUPPORTED THE MAKING OF THIS BOOK; PLEASE SUPPORT AND ENJOY THEM.

ALBURY VINEYARD

Silent Pool
Shere Road
Albury GU5 9BW
Telephone: 01483 229159
Website: www.alburyvineyard.com
Fine wines from the Surrey Hills.

BAKE WITH JACK

Telephone: 07840 561635
Website: www.bakewithjack.co.uk
Helping you bake amazing bread at home via public workshops and private courses at home.

BIRTLEY HOUSE

Bramley
Guildford GU5 0LB
Telephone: 01483 892055
Website: www.birtleyhouse.co.uk
Nursing Home in Surrey since 1932 – dedicated to providing the highest levels of personalised care.

BROWN BAG CRISPS

Terminal House
Station Approach
Shepperton TW17 8AS
Telephone: 01932 569359
Website: www.brownbagcrisps.co.uk
Find us on Twitter, Facebook and
Instagram @brownbagcrisps
We love potato crisps so much that we set out to make the best crisps available! Run by a husband and wife team from Shepperton, we are proud to be Surrey's only brand of potato crisps.

BUBBLE N TWIST ALCHEMY SERVICES

7 Leather Lane
Guildford GU5 9NB
Telephone: 07827 227956
Website: www.bubblentwist.com
Local drink and bar solution for any event, offering Guildford and the villages a friendly, personal and knowledgeable mobile bar service with a twist.

CHEZ VOUS RESTAURANT

432 Limpsfield Road
Warlingham CR6 9LA
Telephone: 01883 620451
Website: www.chezvous.co.uk
Independent local restaurant with a French Heritage combined with strong British roots, featuring unique dishes influenced by traditional cooking and modern trends.

THE COOKIE BAR

1 Royal Parade
Tilford Road
Hindhead GU26 6TD
Telephone: 01428 608001
Website: www.thecookiebar.co.uk
The Cookie Bar is a unique coffee shop, run as a social enterprise business.

CRUMBS BREWING

Cockshot Road
Reigate RH2 7HD
Telephone: 07801 045864
Website: www.crumbsbrewing.co.uk
Crumbs Brewing make beer using leftover artisan bread from Chalk Hills Bakery in Reigate.

DASTAAN INDIAN RESTAURANT

447 Kingston Road
Epsom KT19 0DN
Website: dastaan.co.uk
Telephone: 0208 786 8999
Authentic Indian restaurant with a Bib Gourmand, serving a variety of street food and an amazing set of kebabs and chops. Booking is essential to avoid any disappointments.

THE DORKING BUTCHERY

48 High Street
Dorking RH4 1AY
Telephone: 01306 640517
Website: www.thedorkingbutchery.co.uk
Speciality butchers supplying excellent locally produced meat and dry-aged rare breed beef, with traditional service and a passion for high-quality British produce.

THE DRUNKEN MOUSE

Based in Woking
Telephone: 07976 029573
Website: www.thedrunkenmouse.co.uk
Instagram: @the_drunken_mouse
Facebook: @TheDrunkenMouse
Twitter: Drunken_Mouse1
Caterers specialising in all things cheese and booze related; including pop-up cheese and wine tasting evenings, epic festival toasties with a cider, fine-dining dinner parties and anything else you're hungry for. We operate out of our very own converted horse box and within some of the coolest venues in Surrey.

ELSTEAD VILLAGE DISTILLERS

Thundry Farm
Farnham Road
Elstead
Godalming GU8 6LE, UK
Telephone: 01252 703658
Website: www.elsteadvillagedistillers.com
Small-batch gin producer making four gins from a farm in the Surrey Hills.

GREYFRIARS VINEYARD

The Hog's Back
Puttenham GU3 1AG
Telephone: 01483 813712
Website: www.greyfriarsvineyard.co.uk
Surrey vineyard featuring events and wine tasting experiences.

MANDIRA'S KITCHEN

Silent Pool
Shere Road
Albury
Guildford GU5 9BW
Telephone: 01483 940789
Website: mandiraskitchen.com
Surrey's one-stop shop for delicious ready meals, catering, supper clubs and more, all made with love to authentic Indian recipes.

MISS POLLY CAFÉ

119 Walton Road
East Molesey KT8 0DT
Telephone: 0208 616 2820
Website: www.misspollycafe.co.uk
Find us on Facebook and Instagram @misspollycafe.co.uk
Friendly and family run café, events and catering service
providing restaurant quality food made from high quality, local
produce.

THE RED LION PUB & DINING

Russell Road
Shepperton TW17 9HX
Telephone: 01932 244526
Website: www.redlionshepperton.com
True village pub offering superb seasonal dining, putting honest
food and drink centre stage. The Red Lion boasts a river garden
and bar, plus takeaway fish and chips on Fridays.

THE SALT BOX

Red Oak Barn
Sandy Lane
South Nutfield RH14EJ
Telephone: 07717 319425
Website: www.wearethesaltbox.co.uk
Woodland cookery school and open-fire dining events.

SECRETTS OF MILFORD

Hurst Farm
Chapel Lane
Milford GU8 5HU
Telephone: 01483 520500
Website: www.secretts.co.uk
Award-winning farm shop and pick-your-own featuring the finest
produce fresh from our fields alongside a veritable feast of local
food and drink. A must visit destination for any food lover!

SILENT POOL DISTILLERY

Shere Road
Albury GU5 9BW
Telephone: 01483 229136
Website: silentpooldistillers.com
Email: office@silentpooldistillers.com
Find us on social media @silentpoolgin
Silent Pool Gin is handcrafted at our small distillery in Albury,
Surrey. Our distillery shop is open seven days a week and we
also run public and private tours (booking essential).

SURREY FOOD FESTIVAL

Telephone: 0203 355 5480
Website: www.thelocalfoodfestival.com
Surrey Food Festival offers a great day out and the opportunity
to sample all kinds of cuisines, freshly prepared by the very best
food stalls in the southeast.

WELL SEASONED KITCHEN

7 Coniston Road
Woking GU22 9HU
Telephone: 07980 560391
Website: www.wellseasonedkitchen.co.uk
Find us on Facebook and Instagram @wellseasonedkitchen
Well Seasoned Kitchen creates delicious seasonal food from
the finest home grown and locally sourced produce. Find us at
farmers' markets, farm shops and catered events across Surrey.

THE WISLEY

Ripley
Woking GU23 6QU
Telephone: 01483 211022
Website: www.thewisley.com
A haven for golfers with a passion for the game, featuring a
restaurant with a passion for relaxed fine dining.

OTHER TITLES AVAILABLE

The Little Book of Cakes & Bakes

Featuring recipes and stories from the kitchens of some of the nation's best bakers and cake-makers.
9781910863480

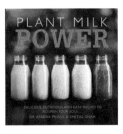

Plant Milk Power

How to create your own delicious, nutritious and nourishing moo-free milks and smoothies.
9781910863411

Whirlow Hall Farm Cook Book

This charity cook book features recipes and stories from staff, local restaurants and supporters to provide a little local inspiration for some simple recipes.
9781910863534

Taste & Tales

This lovingly-created cook book is a beautiful collection of authentic home recipes, inspiring thoughts and heartfelt stories from refugees from the Middle East and Africa.
9781910863596

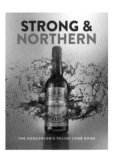

Strong & Northern

The second Henderson's Relish Cook Book reminds us how people use Hendo's every day: splashing over their favourite meals, whether that's a proper pie or Friday fish and chips. 9781910863527

RECENT TITLES FROM OUR 'GET STUCK IN' SERIES

The Bristol and Bath Cook Book features Pinkmans Bakery, featured in The Sunday Times Top 25 bakeries in the UK, The Fish Shop and steak specialists Pasture.
9781910863558

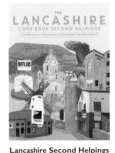

Lancashire Second Helpings
Features acclaimed-Lancastrian Steve Smith from the Freemasons at Wiswell, local favourite The Cartford Inn, award-winning Cuckoo Gin and events from Visit Lancashire.
9781910863510

The Cornish Cook Book
Featuring Gylly Beach, winner of 'Best Café' in the Southwest 2018, The Rising Sun, Cornwall Life's Pub of the Year and Edie's Kitchen run by Nigel Brown.
978-1-910863-47-3

The Edinburgh and East Coast Cook Book
features Masterchef winner Jamie Scott at The Newport, Fhior, Pickering's Gin, Pie Not, Stockbridge Market and much more.
978-1-910863-45-9

The Glasgow and West Coast Cook Book
features The Gannet, Two Fat Ladies, The Spanish Butcher, Hutchesons City Grill, Gamba and much more.
978-1-910863-43-5

The Bristol Cook Book
features Dean Edwards, Lido, Clifton Sausage, The Ox, and wines from Corks of Cotham plus lots more.
978-1-910863-14-5

The Cambridgeshire Cook Book: Second Helpings
features Mark Abbott of Midsummer House, The Olive Grove, Elder Street Café and much more.
978-1-910863-33-6

The Manchester Cook Book: Second Helpings
features Ben Mounsey of Grafene, Hatch, Refuge, Masons, Old School BBQ Bus and much more.
978-1-910863-44-2

The Bath Cook Book
features more than 40 recipes from The Chequers, Hare & Hounds, The Beaufort and Blue Quails Deli plus much more.
9781910863176

The Derbyshire Cook Book: Second Helpings
features Chris Mapp at The Tickled Trout, Chatsworth Farm Shop, Michelin-starred Fischer's, Peacock and much more.
978-1-910863-34-3

All our books are available from Waterstones, Amazon and good independent bookshops.
FIND OUT MORE ABOUT US AT WWW.MEZEPUBLISHING.CO.UK